UNDERSTANDING

EQUINE ACUPUNCTURE

YOUR **GUIDE** TO HORSE HEALTH
CARE AND MANAGEMENT

UNDERSTANDING

EQUINE
ACUPUNCTURE

YOUR **GUIDE** TO HORSE HEALTH
CARE AND MANAGEMENT

By Rhonda Rathgeber, DVM, PhD
Foreword by William H. McCormick, VMD

The Blood-Horse, Inc. Lexington, KY

physical examination, nerve blocks in the case of lameness, and subsequent diagnostic procedures such as radiography, thermography, or nuclear scintigraphy, etc. Lastly some therapy, usually involving drug administration, would follow. There is no guarantee of either a diagnosis or a successful therapy, given that most Western technology is best suited to cases of disease or definitive pain, i.e. lameness. Such a case would correspond to the Chinese disease categories of Bi Syndrome (i.e. extremity pain) and/or low back pain. A TCM physical examination, subsequent to the history and observation of gait, would most probably reveal palpable sites of abnormal musculoskeletal reactivity that would allow categorization of the pattern(s) according to the channel(s) or paths of *Qi* flow; *Qi* being roughly translated as "life forces." An acupuncturist would describe the case in the following way: Pathogenic Wind-Cold have entered the channels resulting in *Qi* Stagnation and to a lesser extent Blood Stasis necessitating the use of the therapeutic principles of Dispelling Wind, Warming the Channels, Moving the Blood, and Rectifying the *Qi*.

That the channel pathways are not part of the Western medical description is irrelevant. For the acupuncturist, the significance of the findings of abnormal pattern rather than disease, led to a therapeutic principle, a consistent course of action within the logic of TCM. Therefore, if *Qi* flow were to be determined to be abnormal in one or more channels, then the practitioner would be committed to use acupoints and medicinals that would have a direct therapeutic effect on the implicated channels.

If the above stated case were not lame and was required to perform in a drug-free competition, such as FEI, or under European racing rules, then one would have a good chance of making a significant therapeutic contribution with acupuncture and herbal medicine. Furthermore, the horse could be noninvasively treated at the time of the examination. Please note that, where permitted, concomitant use of drugs may obscure the effectiveness of TCM treatment, but there would be nothing inherently inconsistent about simultaneous use of these differing therapies. The reason is that the therapeutic principle in TCM is to treat the pattern with a minimization of short- and long-term side effects. In subsequent examinations, the *si jhen* will be used to evaluate the ability of whatever therapy has been used to change the pattern. Lastly, the evaluation of the change in pattern is a strong point of TCM, because it frequently allows the practitioner to predict what a rider may feel in the horse's gait.

Let us consider a second example, that of the Western disease EIPH (Exercise Induced Pulmonary Hemorrhage). Few equine diseases have attracted as much attention from researchers as EIPH. Still, a complete respiratory work up can be expensive and too late. The TCM approach calls for an examination of the patient on a prophylactic basis. Any patient with suspected abnormal bleeding would be grouped in one or a combination of four patterns: Heat, *Qi* vacuity, Blood Stasis, and severance of channels 8. The pattern of pathogenic Heat can be further divided into five categories: Phlegm, Vacuity, Replete, Damp, and Depressive. The practitioner would recognize "Heat" as any physical finding that was red in color as in tracheal hemorrhage, a rapid or forceful pulse, or yellow tracheal phlegm. *Qi* vacuity would be categorized in terms of the abnormal function of the Chinese organ(s) that would be affected. Blood Stasis has several categories as well. Each category will have acupoints and herbal medicinals that have been classically used in therapy to re-establish normal physiological processes. The possible pattern combinations and permutations are legion, and the key to the final formula is the original pattern differential performed by the practitioner using his/her five senses and TCM logic alone. No case ends with treatment; thus, re-evaluation of progress and formula modification are part of the process.

While perusing the following chapters, the reader is asked to remember that therapy in TCM depends on the pattern.

The effectiveness of acupuncture treatment will depend on the practitioner's command of the descriptive methodology and the logic of TCM. What appears to be magic to the Western observer is, in fact, mastery of a myriad of small examinations that results in the logical institution of subsequent therapy. Hopefully, the following chapters will give the reader an appreciation for the practical capability of acupuncture and herbal medicine.

William H. McCormick, VMD

Middleburg, Virginia

Footnotes:

1. Eisenberg, DM et al. "Unconventional Medicine in the United States," *The New England Journal of Medicine*, Vol. 328, No. 4, p. 246-252, 1993 .

2. Jarvis, WT. "Acupuncture, The Position Paper of the National Council Against Health Fraud," *The Clinical Journal of Pain*, Vol. 2, No. 2, p. 162-166, 1991.

3. Ramey, DW. "Do Acupuncture Points and Meridians Actually Exist," *Compendium*, p. 1132-1136, December 2000.

4. Shoen, A, Wynn, S. (eds.) *Complementary and Alternative Veterinary Medicine: Principles and Practice*. St. Louis: Mosby. 1998.

5. Shoen, A. (ed.) *Veterinary Acupuncture, Ancient Art to Modern Medicine*, Goleta, CA.: American Veterinary Publications. 2000.

6. Flaws, B. *The Secret of Chinese Pulse Diagnosis*. Boulder, CO: Blue Poppy Press, p.3, 1995 .

7. Flaws, B. *Sticking To the Point*. Boulder, CO: Blue Poppy Press, p.8, 1990 .

8. Flaws, B. *A Certificate Program in Chinese Medical Herbology*. Boulder, CO: Blue Poppy Seminars, Course 2, p. 69, 1999 .

INTRODUCTION

Igrew up in northern Virginia, where I rode ponies and horses as long as I can remember. I always wanted to be an equine veterinarian, but I never dreamed I also would be doing acupuncture on horses. In fact, my first exposure to acupuncture didn't occur until my senior year of veterinary school when I met Dr. William McCormick, VMD, in Middleburg, Va. He incorporates acupuncture into a very busy lameness practice that uses both Traditional Chinese Medicine and Western medicine. His results using acupuncture intrigued me. He took a great deal of time explaining Chinese theories and drawing meridians to help me understand each case. I was, however, still grasping the finer details of ordinary equine veterinary medicine and felt it inappropriate to take on another "medical profession" at the time.

After graduation I began working at a large equine practice. I have always had a very strong interest in lameness and would get frustrated with some cases that did not respond well to traditional treatment. I wanted to learn more about acupuncture, and after a few years of practice, I signed up to take the course offered by the International Veterinary Acupuncture Society. I wanted to know more, but, once again, I never dreamed I would be doing acupuncture on horses.

To be honest, the course was a lot more than I bargained for. My clients were not happy that I was gone for a week at a time during several months. The course included a practical examination and a written examination that encompassed small-animal information as well as information about birds and cows. I then realized how much I had forgotten about those other species. Also required were a written case report and a number of hours under the supervision of a certified acupuncturist. This meant more time away from a busy practice. Having said all of that, being a certified acupuncturist has been one of the most rewarding aspects of my career. Watching an animal that has not responded to any other form of therapy improve with acupuncture is amazing. Also, introducing people to a different and miraculous medical approach is very satisfying. My hope is this book will contribute to a deeper understanding and acceptance of acupuncture in the Western point of view.

I am extraordinarily lucky to be part of Hagyard-Davidson-McGee, PSC. This first-class equine veterinary practice is the largest of its kind in the world. Presently the practice comprises 39 equine veterinarians. Almost every one of them has referred cases to me for acupuncture. I've been provided the opportunity to work on horses with unusual diseases and to learn more and more every day about the advantages, as well as the disadvantages, of acupuncture. I would not have been able to compose this manuscript without their support. My clients have also contributed to this book by allowing me to use acupuncture on their horses. I have immensely enjoyed introducing acupuncture to them and genuinely appreciate their interest.

Most of the cases I am asked to work on have not responded to Western medicine. The client or referring veterinarian is using acupuncture as a last resort. Therefore, a lot of the cases are very advanced. The fact that acupuncture is effective on most of these advanced cases is a credit to the therapy. I hope that the information presented in this book will encourage people to seek alternative therapies for their horses sooner.

I would like to give a special thanks to the editors of Eclipse Press. Traditional Chinese Medicine is an extremely difficult subject to explain. It took patience and perseverance to help edit this book, and I commend their efforts.

Finally, this book is dedicated to my parents, who bought me my first pony and have since supported my every equine endeavor. I hope one day my husband and I can give our daughter such a lasting gift.

Rhonda Rathgeber, PhD, DVM
Lexington, Kentucky

CHAPTER 1

History of Acupuncture

"It does not matter whether medicine is old or new, so long as it brings about a cure. It matters not whether theories be eastern or western, so long as they prove to be true." — Dr. Jen Hsou Lin, DVM, PhD

Lin's quote underscores how integrating principles of Western medicine and Traditional Chinese Medicine can provide the best treatment for an animal. The Chinese system of healing is termed Traditional Chinese Medicine (TCM) and includes acupuncture, as well as herbs, exercise, diet, and meditation.

The word acupuncture is derived from the Latin words *acus*, meaning "needle," and *pungare*, meaning "to pierce or puncture." Acupuncture is defined as a technique of inserting needles into specific locations on the body for treating certain painful conditions. These specific locations are stimulated and alter various biochemical and physiological parameters to achieve a desired effect.

The development of human acupuncture has been traced to the Stone Age. In general, acupuncture is believed to have originated in China; however, some evidence suggests elementary acupuncture began in northern India or Tibet. Stone instruments called bians were used as acupuncture instruments to relieve pain and disease. Stone bians were replaced with bone or bamboo instruments. Acupuncture in the 16th century through the 11th century B.C. was performed with bronze needles made by bronze casting. These metal needles had bioelectric conductivity, which led to the discovery of channels or meridians within the body.

In approximately 220 B.C., Pien Chueh compiled *Hwang di Nei Jing* or *The Inner Classic of the Yellow Emperor*, a text detailing the basic theories of TCM. It also locates the various acupuncture points and explains different needling techniques. The text also describes how the heart controls the flow of blood throughout the body. William Harvey, an English Royal Physician and the leading anatomist of his day, made this very same discovery in Western medicine in 1628.

Acupuncture flourished until the Ching Dynasty. During this time (about 1880 until 1900) acupuncture was banned for political reasons, and its practitioners were threatened with imprisonment. The rulers of the time thought acupuncture was too simplistic, and they promoted the institution of Western medicine as the only form of health care. The Mao Tse-Tung Communist Party in the 1940s advocated acupuncture again and used it for soldiers injured in the War of Liberation. Both forms of medicine are now practiced in China.

Acupuncture spread to other countries as Western missionaries returned from China. Acupuncture and TCM were touted to the Western world through the writings of James Reston, a correspondent for *The New York Times*. He suffered appendicitis while traveling with Richard Nixon in 1978 after the former president had established a cultural and scientific exchange with the People's Republic of China. After undergoing surgery in a Beijing hospital, Reston was experiencing stomach discomfort. The Chinese premier, Chou En-lai, suggested that he receive acupuncture, and the hospital's specialist inserted needles in Reston's right elbow and below his knees. Within an hour Reston reported that the distension in his stomach had eased. The problem never recurred. During his recuperation, Reston wrote a long account of "this needling," which the *Times* played on the front page.

The explanation of how acupuncture works evolved over thousands of years. But the practice of acupuncture began before writing or record keeping existed. As information accumulated, a system was necessary to recall the knowledge. Over time, a story of events was woven from the observations of the ancient Chinese. The story did not have to be true; it simply had to account for the observations.

It is fascinating to realize how much the Chinese learned by observation and gross dissection. For example, people observed that when someone was hurt in one part of the body, a previous pain in a different part went away or diminished.

Although it is uncertain whether human acupuncture originated in China, India, or Tibet, veterinary acupuncture was used in China during the Shang and Chow dynasties (2000-3000 B.C.) Records include a treatise on elephant acupuncture dating from about 3,000 years ago that was recently discovered in Sri Lanka. The earliest verified record of Chinese veterinary medicine was written during the Shang Dynasty and was entitled *Horse Priests*. It described treating animals by placating evil spirits. Domestication of animals started in China during the 16th to 11th centuries B.C. In a natural progression of man's relationship with domesticated animals, medical treatments used on humans extrapolated into a rudimentary form of veterinary medicine. Written in 650 B.C., the first veterinary textbook, *Bai-le's Canon of Veterinary Medicine* by Sun-Yang, was based on acupuncture. Sun-Yang was a skilled acupuncturist, especially with horses. A legend related in the book says that veterinary acupuncture was mistakenly discovered when lame horses used in battle were found to become sound after being hit by arrows at distinct points. Ancient rock carvings show military horses being "acupunctured" with arrows prior to battle. Since horses were an important part of the economy, it is not surprising that early acupuncture involved horses.

Western equine practitioners have only employed acupuncture in the past three or four decades, almost 50 years after the practice became recognized in the United States. In 1926 *North American Medical and Surgical Journal* published an article entitled "Cases illustrative of the remedial effects of acupuncture." Interest in acupuncture grew as surprising results were observed. In 1974 the Acupuncture Society of America assumed the task of overseeing and regulating the practice of acupuncture in the U.S. One year later the organization became the International Veterinary Acupuncture Society. IVAS remains the leading organization for veterinary acupuncturists around the world.

Acupuncture is the medical treatment of choice for 25 percent of the world's population. More than 800 veterinary acupuncturists practice in the United States and almost every veterinary conference across the country holds continuing education lectures on acupuncture. However, the lack of an easy explanation of how acupuncture works causes many people to question its validity.

A 1998 survey by the American Association of Equine Practitioners Therapeutic Options Task Force showed that 37 percent of its members used acupuncture in their practice. The task force reviewed literature regarding acupuncture to examine it as a therapeutic option. The group used a "peer review" analysis in which veterinarians reviewed 66 papers and rated them based on acupuncture's effectiveness. The group also rated the quality of each paper.

The task force concluded that the reviewed literature supports the use of acupuncture; 75 percent of the papers demonstrated improvement in cases treated with acupuncture. However, the reports received below-average scores relative to other scientific papers because the studies had poor control groups and small numbers of cases.

Based on the results of the task force's review, the AAEP continues to encourage high-quality research by funding grants for acupuncture and other complementary therapies.

CHAPTER 2
General Principles of Acupuncture

Acupuncture can be described as a healing science that deals with the entire individual animal as an energetic being. Acupuncture concentrates on changes in the body's homeostasis (physiological equilibrium) that underlie the presenting symptoms. Western medicine treats the animal's symptoms with medications; acupuncture and Traditional Chinese Medicine treat the whole animal as an entity in its environment. The body is thought to be in harmony with the environment. The neuroendocrine responses (the interaction between the nervous and endocrine systems) achieved by needle insertion are the same ones the body uses to regulate its

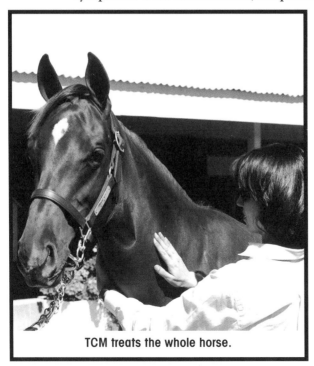

TCM treats the whole horse.

physiological processes. For example, when the body is injured, the brain sends signals to the pituitary gland to secrete substances into the blood stream. These substances will attract certain cell types and mediators to the injured area to aid healing. Acupuncture enhances this signal.

According to the concept of Traditional Chinese Medicine, each animal is born with a fixed amount of energy called *Qi* (pronounced chee). The animal uses energy to live and replenishes this energy with food, water, and air. Blood vessels are used to distribute nutrients. The source of *Qi* is either inherited or environmental. In ancient Chinese philosophy *Qi* is the energy that creates and nourishes life and leaves the body at the time of death. It is not a substance, but an idea or principle of the smooth interaction of rhythmic patterns within the body. It is not something one can see or touch. *Qi* passes along a network of meridians or channels in the body similar to an electric current. The network of meridians connects the internal organs to the exterior of the body. Therefore, *Qi* maintains balance in bodily functions. When disease is present, the energy becomes imbalanced. This disruption of the electrical system short-circuits the body and leads to malfunction.

Acupuncture stimulates certain reflex points to allow the body to balance the energy and heal the disease. Acupuncture points are located along the meridians and serve as booster points, stations, or regulators of energy flow. The points can be near the site of disease or far away from it. The use of needles balances the energy by mediat-

AT A GLANCE

• Acupuncture addresses the whole animal as an energetic being.

• Each individual is thought to be born with a fixed amount of energy called *Qi*.

• When disease is present, the body's internal energy, or *Qi*, becomes imbalanced.

• Acupuncture stimulates certain reflex points that allow the body to become rebalanced.

ing the nervous system, hormones, and humoral factors, which are substances the body produces to regulate the function of certain organs. Some examples of humoral factors are endorphins, cortisol, and immune cells. Stimulation of the nervous system, hormones, and humoral factors will adjust blood flow and affect organ function. It will relieve muscle spasms and allow injuries to heal more readily by increasing blood flow and the ability to remove toxins from the site of injury. Acupuncture causes the release of endorphins and cortisol. These substances can reduce pain and swelling and help build the body's immune system. The basis of acupuncture is the relation of certain areas or points on the surface of the body to specific internal body organs and functions. This is called a somatotrophic relationship between nerves and vessels and their corresponding internal organs, a relationship also recognized by Western studies.

For example, an acupoint on the outside of the last (fifth) toe correlates with the eye and its associated structures. Human patients who had magnetic resonance imaging (MRI) while that point was stimulated with an acupuncture needle showed a significant increase in activity of the entire visual cortex of the brain. The MRI showed a similar reaction when the patients were asked to look at a strong flashing light. Stimulation of points only two to five centimeters away from the acupoint did not show the same activity. Without these benefits of technology, the ancient Chinese could not easily relate form to function as modern scientists can. However, they proposed astounding relationships between organ systems and their biorhythms by simple observation.

When administered by a properly trained veterinarian, acupuncture is one of the safest forms of medical treatments. Some veterinarians have said that acupuncture can shorten the healing process by half. It can be used for diagnosing conditions as well as treating conditions in the horse.

Acupuncture is commonly confused with chiropractic; however, it is not the same as chiropractic. Chiropractic is a therapy based on the relationship among the animal, the spinal column, and the nervous system. Although many certified acupuncturists are also certified in chiropractic, the two forms of therapy are completely separate.

CHAPTER 3
Overview of Traditional Chinese Medicine

Understanding Traditional Chinese Medicine's terminology and metaphors requires study and patience because familiar terms and applications are used in a completely different manner. For example, the Chinese refer to certain diseases as being generated by "Heat," "Wind," or "Dampness." Western medicine does not recognize "Dampness," yet it can treat what the Chinese refer to as Dampness of the Spleen. The Western equivalent of Dampness of the Spleen is colic with yellow diarrhea. Western Medicine does not recognize "Wind," but can treat what the Chinese call Liver Wind, the rapid onset of convulsions.

Traditional Chinese Medicine explains health and disease using several symbolic systems that can be applied to both humans and horses. This form of medicine was derived from conceptual notions that invoke ideas about the environment in which the body moves and lives. The external environment includes nutrition, temperature, humidity, air quality, social factors, seasonal influences, and diurnal influences. Because Western medicine is based on the belief that illness is explained by physical and biological factors, it treats the signs of disease and not the entire body.

Traditional Chinese Medicine is more dynamic, with patterns of disease and no causal relationships. The patient's medical history is also different.

Evaluations correspond to the Five Elements and Eight Principle theories of TCM. In addition to the questions the veterinarian may ask the owner of the horse, other important questions are asked:

Does the animal drink a lot or play in the water bucket? The greater the thirst, the more internal heat has accrued. This can occur from a deficiency in the body fluids or be secondary to infection.

> ## AT A GLANCE
>
> • TCM explains health and disease using several symbolic systems.
>
> • Evaluations correspond to the Five Element and Eight Principle theories of TCM.
>
> • TCM is based on the theory of opposites.
>
> • The opposites are paired and called Yin and Yang.

Does the animal have a temperature preference? Standing in the hot sun as opposed to in a shelter or not wanting to leave the barn in the winter are examples of horses that are seeking warmth. This indicates a Yang deficiency. Horses that do not perform well in the heat may have a Yin deficiency.

Does the animal have softer than normal manure or appear constipated, having hard fecal balls? Diarrhea may indicate a Spleen imbalance, a Liver imbalance, or a Kidney Yang deficiency. Constipation may be related to dryness from the Lung or to moisture imbalance of the Spleen.

Does the condition occur at a specific time of day or a particular time of the year? This may be related to the flow of *Qi* in certain organs during specific times of the day. The Five Elements are also paired with the different seasons so that a condition that occurs in the summer may be related to the Heart or Small Intestine.

The physical examination of the horse differs from the Western medical examination. The color of the tongue, the smell, pulse quality, hair coat, temperament, and body type are all used in the TCM examination. Specific acupuncture points are palpated, and the response at each point is recorded and correlated with a TCM diagnosis.

The goal of both types of practice is to establish a healthy, homeostatic patient. One practice does not have to replace the other. A horse suffering from a hock problem may benefit from acupuncture as well as intra-articular therapy and anti-inflammatory agents.

Traditional Chinese Medicine is based on the theory of opposites, whose interaction creates the energy called *Qi*. The energy travels through channels in the body called meridians. Acupuncture points along the channels can affect the flow of energy through the meridians. The practitioner can influence the flow of *Qi* at these points. Hence, if an organ has too much energy, it can be treated by decreasing the flow of energy into the organ or by increasing the flow of energy out of it. Or vice versa.

Dr. Joyce Harmon, DVM, MRCVS, a leading practitioner of alternative therapies, compares acupuncture to a bio-electric system. Each acupuncture point is like a dimmer switch. If there is disease, the flow in the system is interrupted, and the dimmer switch is turned down so that less electricity passes through. When the patient is treated with acupuncture, the dimmer switch is turned up again and allows the electricity to flow normally again.

The source of *Qi* is either inherited or environmental. *Qi* is derived from prenatal sources (inherited) and from the food and water the horse eats and the air the animal breathes (environmental). *Qi* has five functions. It transforms, transports, warms, protects, and holds the fluids in place. Disease blocks, reverses, restricts, or weakens the flow of *Qi*. Decreased *Qi* in one particular organ may lead to increased or excess *Qi* in another organ. These situations may present themselves as different patterns or signs in the animal.

The opposites are paired and are called Yin and Yang. In Traditional Chinese Medicine, everything is paired with its relative opposite. Yin–Yang philosophy teaches not only that two opposites can exist simultaneously, but also that the very existence of each depends on the presence of the other.

They mutually consume and produce one another, and they are in a constant state of dynamic balance. Yin and Yang represent the shady and sunny sides of a mountain. Yin is shade or darkness; Yang is light or brightness. This also can be translated to night (Yin) and day (Yang). The cyclic nature of night and day also leads to the understanding of the relativity of Yin and Yang. Midnight is the utmost Yin. As the night becomes morning and the day approaches, Yang increases until it reaches its highest point at noon. Yin is at its lowest point at this time, but begins to increase as dusk approaches. The cycle keeps repeating. Therefore, Yin and Yang control each other and actually transform into each other.

Yin can be thought of as matter, and Yang can be thought of as the spirit. For example, blood is Yin and *Qi* is Yang. Blood is matter, and *Qi* is the energy to circulate blood or move the matter. Yin includes negative, inside, ventral, north, female, parasympathetic nervous system, chronic diseases, and counterclockwise. Yang includes positive, outside, dorsal, south, male, sympathetic nervous system, acute diseases, and clockwise. A constant rhythm cycles between Yin and Yang. An imbalance between this cycling shifts either Yin or Yang. A shift toward Yang results in overactivity while a shift toward Yin results in underactivity. Yin and Yang are associated with every organ in the body.

CHINESE THEORIES

Two different Chinese medical theories have developed over the centuries: the Five Element Theory and the Eight Principle Theory. The Five Element Theory can describe a general or specific state of imbalance. The Eight Principle Theory describes disease by a specific set of symptoms. The two systems are not mutually exclusive, and they both attempt to describe and explain observable phenomenon. Different practitioners use the different methods for different cases, and they get equal results. Some cases are better described by the Five Element Theory, and others are best described using the Eight Principle Theory.

FIVE ELEMENT THEORY

The theory of the Five Elements is based on the concept that everything in the universe is the product of movement and change of the five basic elements and their growth cycles. The five elements are Wood, Fire, Earth, Metal, and Water. One must remember that this theory is based on analogy and the terms are not literal. Each element represents a certain quality and stage of transformation and is regulated by a negative feedback system and a control system. Each of the five organ systems is represented by a symbol: Wood is a symbol for the liver. Fire is the heart. Earth represents the spleen. Metal is the lung. Water represents the kidney. The organ system is not the anatomical organs but the Traditional Chinese Medicine organs. TCM organs are named according to their function and not their gross anatomy. For example, the Lung in TCM controls and receives *Qi*.

The five elements are not static concepts but components of normal growth, function, and development. Each element must exist in harmony with the others for the organism to enjoy dynamic balance. Each element or phase is part of a larger, more ordered transformation cycle where nothing is static. There is a cycle of creation or production called the Sheng cycle. A certain phase produces the next phase. The Fire produces the Earth, Earth produces Metal, Metal produces Water, Water produces Wood, and Wood produces Fire. When the Fire burns, it produces ashes, which then go in the Earth. From the Earth, ore is made into Metal. The Metal is melted to give off steam and become Water. Wood is produced from the Water, as vegetation needs water to grow. The Wood is burned to make Fire and complete the creation cycle. This cycle is controlled by a separate cycle to keep balance referred to as the destruction cycle or the Ko cycle. Wood can destroy the earth by erupting its roots or covering the earth with its leaves. Earth destroys Water by damming the flow of Water or absorbing it in the ground. Water destroys Fire, and Fire destroys or melts Metal. Metal destroys Wood by chopping it down.

The Five Element theory is used to locate an imbalance. In TCM, the Five Elements are used to categorize organs, tissues, senses, colors, seasons, and emotions. When disease is present, the cycles and their associated organs interact. For example, diseases of the stomach (Earth) can transfer to disorders of the heart (Fire). Given the correlations among the elements and the sense organs — tastes, emotions, seasons, colors, environmental factors, and tissues — Traditional Chinese Medicine uses this theory to assess the patient. A pattern of liver blood deficiency may cause weakness in tendons and dryness in the hooves. A pattern of liver excess may produce bloodshot eyes and an angry temperament. Different patterns are more prevalent in different seasons or weather conditions.

THE SHENG OR CREATION CYCLE

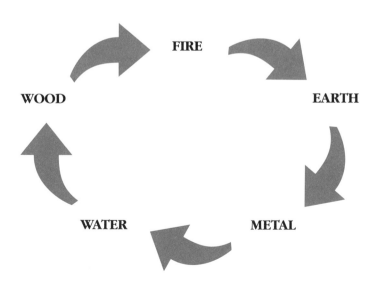

THE KO OR DESTRUCTION CYCLE

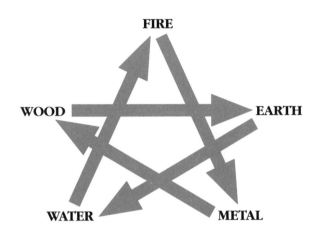

	WOOD	**FIRE**	**EARTH**	**METAL**	**WATER**
Yin Organ	Liver	Heart	Spleen	Lung	Kidney
Yang Organ	Gall Bladder	Small Intestine	Stomach	Large Intestine	Bladder
Sense Organ	Eyes	Tongue	Mouth	Nose	Ears
Tissue	Tendons	Blood Vessels	Flesh	Skin	Bones
Season	Spring	Summer	Indian Summer	Fall	Winter
Emotion	Anger	Joy	Worry	Grief	Fear
Transition	Birth	Growth	Maturity	Harvest	Storage

EIGHT PRINCIPLE THEORY

The Eight Principle theory is based on different patterns of disease.

<u>Eight Principles</u>

Yin	Yang
Interior	Exterior
Deficiency	Excess
Cold	Hot

A refinement of the Yin-Yang philosophy, the Eight Principle Theory is a model for organizing symptoms and signs into diagnostic categories. The categories include heat/cold, interior/exterior, Yin/Yang, excess/deficiency, and several combinations of these. The patient is evaluated according to the four examinations: looking, listening, asking, and touching. The practitioner would look for different signs as compared with a Western doctor. The signs would include when the condition first occurred, triggering factors, energy level, hot or cold sensations, muscle weakness, respiration, tongue coat, pulse, skin, voice, sleeping patterns, and movements. The signs are then categorized into a paradigm that fulfills the criteria of these categories.

The Eight Principle theory is best illustrated by a clinical example. Two horses present with a lack of appetite and mild recurring colic. A Western veterinarian diagnoses the two horses with stomach ulcers by performing an endoscopic examination. Each horse is treated with anti-ulcer medication. A Traditional Chinese Medicine veterinarian examines each horse and diagnoses two separate conditions. The first horse is thin with a poor hair coat. Her groom comments that she drinks a lot of water and has a tendency to have hard manure. She is very nervous during the examination. Her tongue is dry and slightly red. Her pulse is "thin" and "fast." This horse is said to have the pattern of "Deficient Yin Affecting the Stomach."

The second horse has severe cramping or colic on a regular basis. His movement is heavy and slow. He is quiet but does not like to be touched on his abdomen. He has a tendency toward loose manure. His tongue has a very thick, white, moist coating; his pulse is "tight" and "slippery." These signs lead to a diagnosis of the pattern of "Excess Cold Dampness Affecting the Spleen and Stomach." The TCM doctor would treat this by doing acupuncture (possibly using moxibustion) on the Spleen and Stomach meridians to "warm and dry" the meridian. As illustrated, the TCM doctor searches for and organizes signs that a Western doctor does not recognize. Each patient is assessed differently and treated differently even though it may have the same disease process by Western standards.

The body has the ability to resist the invasion of various pathogenic factors to keep a relative balance within the body and between the body and the environment. This ability is named "anti-pathogenic *Qi*." Disease occurs when pathogens overcome the body's anti-pathogenic *Qi* and disrupts the balance within the body or the balance between the body and the environment. This also disrupts the Yin and Yang in the body and presents itself accordingly. Therefore, when the anti-pathogenic factor is strong, the invasion of pathogens is less likely. If the pathogens invade the body, it usually means that the anti-pathogenic factor is weak or insufficient. Therefore, TCM tries to treat this factor to keep it strong.

Acupuncture is effective because it regulates and improves the defensive function of the anti-pathogenic factor. The pathogens can be Wind, Cold, Summer Heat, Dampness, Dryness, and Heat and can be directly associated with disease. The vital activities of the body are thought to be closely related to changes in weather. The significance of the pathogens is based on the clinical manifestation and not necessarily the nature or degree of pathogen. The clinical manifestation is recognized as the "pattern" in TCM. There are external patterns as just described, and there are internal patterns. Internal patterns are usually more chronic diseases and arise from a disruption of homeostasis (equilibrium) within the body systems.

CHAPTER 4

Acupuncture Points

Acupuncture stimulates a specific point on the horse's body to achieve a therapeutic effect. These points or acupoints are called *Shu Xue. Shu* means "communication or passing," and *Xue* means "a hole or an outlet." In Traditional Chinese acupuncture, *Shu Xue* translates as a hole in the skin that communicates with one or more internal organs.

The horse's body has 361 acupoints. These were located first on human beings and then anatomically transposed to the horse. This task was more difficult than it seems because of anatomical differences. For example, the horse's hoof corresponds to a single digit, or toe, in the human rather than five digits. Hence the location of some points is not definitive.

To describe the exact location of particular points, both human and equine practitioners use a unit of measurement known as a *tsun (cun)*. It is proportional to the size of the animal and helps describe the exact location of particular points. One *tsun* is approximately the width of a single rib of the animal. In the horse this would be roughly equivalent to the width of two fingers, while in the pony one *tsun* is approximately the width of one finger.

Acupuncture points lie along meridians and pathways of major peripheral nerves. They correspond to known neural structures: motor nerves, superficial nerves, nerve plexi, and muscle-tendon junctions called golgi tendon organs. Acupuncture uses these neural structures to achieve its therapeutic effects. Therefore, if the nerves are damaged, the effects of acupuncture may be slow or decreased.

The insertion of the needle causes surprisingly little sensitivity despite an increased number of nerves and vessels at each acupoint. In fact, most horses will relax once the needle is in place. Anesthetizing the area of insertion will hinder the benefits of acupuncture. Acupuncture is,

AT A GLANCE

• Acupuncture stimulates a specific point on a horse's body to achieve a therapeutic effect.

• The horse's body has 361 acupoints.

• Acupuncture points lie along meridians and pathways of major peripheral nerves. They correspond to known neural structures.

• Insertion of needles at acupoints causes little or no discomfort.

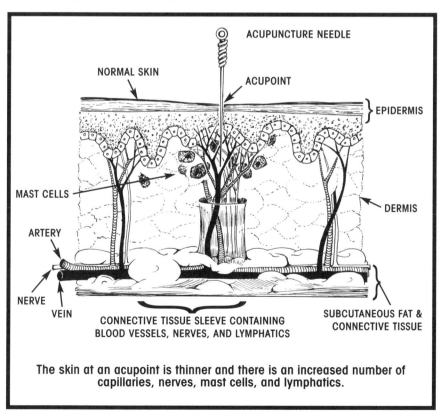

ACUPUNCTURE NEEDLE

NORMAL SKIN

ACUPOINT

EPIDERMIS

MAST CELLS

DERMIS

ARTERY

NERVE

VEIN

CONNECTIVE TISSUE SLEEVE CONTAINING BLOOD VESSELS, NERVES, AND LYMPHATICS

SUBCUTANEOUS FAT & CONNECTIVE TISSUE

The skin at an acupoint is thinner and there is an increased number of capillaries, nerves, mast cells, and lymphatics.

therefore, mediated in part through the nervous system, including both the somatic and autonomic nervous systems. The somatic nervous system includes nerves that control voluntary muscular movement and allow the body to be aware of its movements. The autonomic nervous system serves body functions that are subconscious or involuntary, such as movement of food through the gastrointestinal tract and the rhythmic pumping of the heart.

Acupuncture points have several properties, including more capillaries, arterioles, fine lymphatic vessels, mast cells, free nerve endings, and nerve fibers. The skin is slightly thinner at acupoints, and there is increased blood circulation. These properties make acupoints extremely reactive to the microscopic damage of needle insertion. Electrical resistance or impedance is decreased at acupoints, meaning that electricity flows more readily at acupoints as compared to the surrounding skin. The points can be electrically measured objectively with a galvanic device called an ohmmeter, which measures electrical potential on the skin. A wide range of errors can occur, however, if one relies solely on this method of diagnosis. Variations in the readings occur with the sensitivity of the device, the physiology of the animal, the environment or climate, and the measuring technique. Decreased electrical impedance at acupoints remains measurable on amputated limbs, cadavers, and removed animal skin. This supports the fact that this phenomenon is electrical and not biological. It does not require a blood supply to exist.

At acupoints, diseased patients have skin electrical potential that is specifically related to a particular disorder. When a horse has a disease or injury, the electrical potential at specific points is different, usually less, than when the disease is not present. This can be proven by the changing electrical potential at acupoints when disease is experimentally induced. For example, electrical potential was reduced in certain stomach meridian points after an experimental transection of the vagus nerve called a vagotomy. This nerve originates in the brain and innervates several internal organs, including the intestines. It is responsible for the constant peristalsis or movement of the gastrointestinal tract. When the nerve is transected, there is no control of gastrointestinal motility and the GI tract shuts down. This is called GI atony, a common condition following colic surgery in the horse. When the gastrointestinal tract shuts down, the bacteria that normally remain within the guts are absorbed into the bloodstream. This can result in laminitis and fatal shock. Skin resistance and electrical potential distinctly lessened at the acupoints after the vagotomy. Acupuncture actually has been shown to minimize the change or reduction in skin resistance and significantly improve the post-vagotomy gastrointestinal atony (decreased motility). It stimulates the gastrointestinal tract to return to its normal motility after surgery. Acupuncture does this by its so-called viscerosomatic effect, which stimulates other nerves that supply the internal organs.

An interesting Russian study illustrates the principle of *Shu Xue*: a "hole in the skin that communicates with another part of the body." Medical technologists tested the hypothesis that acupoints in the hind leg communicate to other areas of the body. They used rabbits for the experiment. Formaldehyde was injected into an acupoint on the front of the hind leg. Formaldehyde will irritate tissues and cause inflammation at the injection site. Dye was then injected into the vein. The dye will localize in areas of inflammation. The dye was introduced into the circulation to see if there was inflammation at sites other than the injection site. The dye showed up in the ears of the rabbits. This finding indicates a relationship between the point of injection and another part of the body far removed from the original site of injection, namely the ear. If the formaldehyde was then injected into an acupoint on the back of the hind leg, the dye in the blood showed up in a separate point on the ear. This is just one example of how acupoints communicate with areas distant to the point location.

ACUPOINT CATEGORIES

Traditional Chinese Medicine has many different categories of acupoints. The acupuncturist must strategically use different acupoints to achieve the desired effects. Some types of points are used to increase energy or *Qi* in the meridian while other points are used to decrease *Qi* in the meridian. Different categories of acupoints are used for diseases involving the organs while other points are more specific for musculoskeletal problems. It should be noted that there is obviously more than one approach to TCM, and different practitioners will approach a problem differently. The same applies to Western medicine. The most frequently used acupoint categories are discussed below.

Ting points

Ting points are the beginning or ending points of a meridian, where energy is exchanged with the exterior. They are very powerful points to balance energy. The *Ting* points in

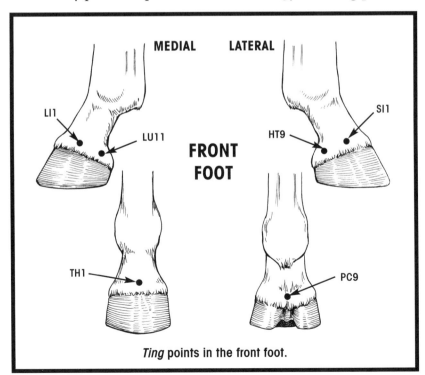

Ting points in the front foot.

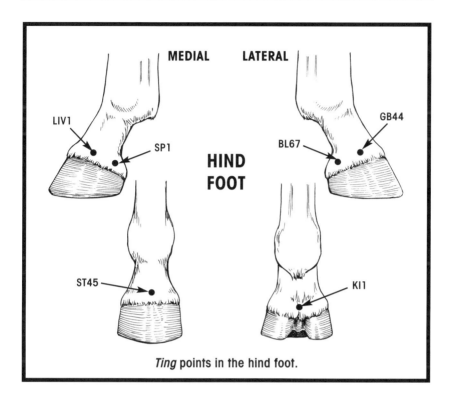

Ting points in the hind foot.

the horse are all on the coronary band. Some meridians begin with the *Ting* point, while some meridians end with the *Ting* point. *Ting* points are points of energy interchange as well as of transference of energy to the paired meridian. The flow of *Qi* follows a set pathway through each meridian. If flow is interrupted in one meridian due to disease or injury, the flow in other meridians may be altered. The meridians are paired with a Yin meridian and a Yang meridian together. If one of the meridians in the pair becomes imbalanced, the *Ting* point of the other meridian may be a good treatment point to help transfer that energy.

Association Points

Association points or *Shu* points relate to an anatomical structure along the meridian pathway. These points act as indicators to help identify where the imbalance resides on the body. *Shu* points are extremely important in acupuncture diagnosis. Generally, if an Association point is sensitive to light pressure it may indicate an acute condition. If the point is painful with deep pressure, it usually indicates a chronic condition. The 12 Association points are located along the inner branch of the Bladder meridian between the withers and the tail. They are two to four inches away from the spine.

Alarm Points

Alarm points or *Mu* points relate specifically to a particular organ. Sensitivity at an Alarm point indicates a problem with the organ for which it is named. *Mu* translates literally to "collecting," meaning points where *Qi* collects. They are located on the abdomen and chest. They are most often used diagnostically. In human medicine, McBurney's point is a type of "alarm point." It corresponds with the normal position of the base of the appendix and displays special tenderness in cases of appendicitis. It corresponds to a point on the Stomach meridian (ST25) in Traditional Chinese Medicine.

Local (Trigger) Points

Local points (*Ahshi* points), also sometimes called Trigger points, are more sensitive when there is a local injury. They may or may not lie on a meridian. They are only apparent when there is an injury. If a horse falls over a jump, the next day he is usually very sore. Palpation of his neck and back is likely to reveal very sore "Trigger points" from local bruising. Horses usually get relief from deep massage or acupuncture of these points.

Master Points

Master points affect large anatomical or functional areas such as the head and neck or the face and mouth. These points are used for problems within the region of influence of each point. There are six Master points specific for six anatomical areas. For example, the Master point for the head and neck may be used for a horse that has a sinus infection.

MASTER POINT	ANATOMICAL AREA
LI4	Face and Mouth
LU7	Head and Neck
ST36	Abdomen and GI Tract
SP6	Urogenital System
BL40	Back and Hips
PC6	Chest

Stimulation Points

Stimulation points, also referred to as Tonification points, increase energy flow on the meridian for which it is named. If an older mare is having reproductive problems, she is said to have Deficient Kidney *Qi* because in TCM the Kidney regulates fertility. Treatment would involve acupuncture of the Kidney Stimulation point.

Sedation Points

Sedation points are used selectively to decrease energy level in a specific meridian or organ. They are used to treat "excess" conditions by dispersing the excess energy within the meridian flow. A horse that has a temper can be treated by sedating the Liver because the Liver is associated with anger.

Source Points

Source points or *Yuan* points store "source *Qi*" and are located on each of the 12 meridians. The Source point is directly connected to an organ's meridian. They are commonly used in treating diseases of the Yin Organs. All Source points are near the knee or hock on the horse. A noticeable swelling or concavity at an acupoint indicates the need for Source point treatment, which can produce an immediate effect. If the horse has a respiratory problem, stimulation of the Lung Source point can help bring the Lung meridian into balance.

Connecting Points

Each of the major meridians communicates with its paired channel through the Connecting point or *Luo* point. These points can, therefore, be used to treat disorders of both Yin and Yang meridians by equalizing *Qi* between coupled channels. The Connecting points behave as "short-circuits," allowing for excess of energy to pass through the point from one channel to another. For instance, disharmony in the Stomach meridian can be balanced by treating the Spleen Connecting point. Connecting points are most commonly used in conjunction with the Source points. For example, a horse with weak or deficient lungs may need tonification of the Lung Source point and sedation of the Connecting point of the Lung with the Large Intestine.

Horory Points

Horory points are the most powerful points on each meridian at a particular time of day as related to the circadian clock. The greatest concentration of *Qi* in the meridian will be found at this point during the meridian's peak activity. As such, when this point is stimulated during the time of day that the meridian is receiving its greatest energy, the effects of treatment are enhanced.

Accumulation Points

Accumulation points are also called *Xi-Cleft* points. These are points where *Qi* and Blood tend to naturally accumulate. They are used to treat acute diseases by relieving obstructions in the meridian.

Influential Points

Influential points have strong effects on functional systems such as the bones, ligaments, and tendons. These points are used in conjunction with other points.

Auricular Points

Points on the ear that correspond to different parts of the body are used in Auricular acupuncture. Acupuncturists commonly use these points to help people quit smoking by placing an implant in the point in the ear.

The acupuncturist may use these acupoint categories in a variety of combinations. The combination depends on the disease, the acupuncture examination, personal preference, and the temperament of the horse. If a certain combination of points is not effective, then an alternate combination should be used.

CHAPTER 5
What is a Meridian or Channel?

Meridians are a network of channels that regulate body functions. In Traditional Chinese Medicine, all body parts are interconnected by the network and their associated secondary channels.

Twelve bilateral meridians are each paired with the 12 internal organs of the body: the lung, large intestine, stomach, spleen, heart, small intestine, bladder, kidney, pericardium, triple heater, gall bladder, and liver. Each paired meridian courses along both sides of the body. In Traditional Chinese Medicine these organs are defined by their functions and not their physical structure; therefore, organs exist in Traditional Chinese Medicine that do not exist in Western medicine, such as the Triple Heater meridian. The Triple Heater is a function and not an actual organ and has no equivalent in Western medicine. It is the functional relationship of several organs. It transforms and transports *Qi* as it flows through the body. There are also eight extra channels that are not associated with internal organs. They are called unpaired meridians since they are not associated with a particular organ. Two commonly used extra channels are the Governing Vessel and the Conception Vessel. They are important supplements to the 12 paired meridians.

Knowing the relative paths of each meridian allows the veterinarian to diagnose and treat specific conditions appropriately. Diseases associated with a certain organ or its association point may reflect a problem along the course of the particular meridian. For example, an imbalance associated with the Lung meridian may signify pathology along the course of this meridian or pathology of the Lung. The meridian courses from the chest to the inside of the heel. Therefore, a splint on the inside of the horse's leg may cause a reaction in the Lung meridian or its association points.

AT A GLANCE

- Meridians are a network of channels that regulate body function.

- Twelve bilateral meridians are paired with 12 internal organs.

- Eight additional channels are known as unpaired meridians.

- Energy, or *Qi*, flows through the body in a 24-hour cycle via the meridians.

- Stimulating a specific point on the body can stimulate the entire meridian.

The six Yang meridians carry a positive charge. These meridians are illuminated by the sun, according to TCM. Each

THE DIRECTION AND TIME OF MAXIMUM ENERGY FLOW ALONG THE MERIDIANS

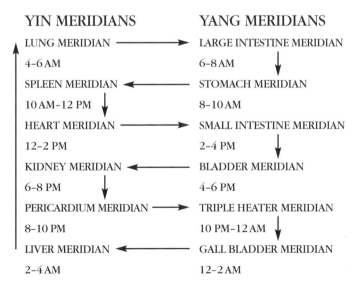

YIN MERIDIANS	YANG MERIDIANS
LUNG MERIDIAN ⟶	LARGE INTESTINE MERIDIAN
4–6 AM	6–8 AM
SPLEEN MERIDIAN ⟵	STOMACH MERIDIAN
10 AM–12 PM	8–10 AM
HEART MERIDIAN ⟶	SMALL INTESTINE MERIDIAN
12–2 PM	2–4 PM
KIDNEY MERIDIAN ⟵	BLADDER MERIDIAN
6–8 PM	4–6 PM
PERICARDIUM MERIDIAN ⟶	TRIPLE HEATER MERIDIAN
8–10 PM	10 PM–12 AM
LIVER MERIDIAN ⟵	GALL BLADDER MERIDIAN
2–4 AM	12–2 AM

Yang meridian has a corresponding Yin meridian that carries a negative charge. These pathways are in the shadows. For example, in the horse three Yin meridians of the forelimb flow from the chest to the foot where they meet three Yang meridians and ascend back to the head. The three Yang meridians of the hind limb start at the head and descend to the hind foot. There they meet three Yin meridians and continue upward to the chest where they join the three Yin meridians of the forelimb. This completes the cycle of energy flow in the body.

Qi circulates throughout the body in a continuous flow, taking 24 hours to pass through all the meridians. There are 12 two-hour time lots when *Qi* is dominant in a particular organ. Trained acupuncturists will use this information when collecting information for the history and diagnosis of the patient. If a patient is painful only during a certain time of the day, the meridian that is most active at that time may be involved in the diagnosis and treatment. For example, the fact that a racehorse coughs only when the groom arrives at the stable at 5 a.m. may be significant to the TCM practitioner's diagnosis. If practical, this may be the best time frame to treat the horse with acupuncture because the maximal *Qi* or energy is in the meridian at this time.

Although meridians are difficult to visualize, there are instances when they are apparent to the naked eye. There have been reports of human dermatosis or skin diseases along the the exact channel of certain meridians. The skin diseases include neurodermatitis, lichen planus, linear scleroderma, nervus anemicus, and sebaceous dermatitis.

One of the most fascinating phenomenon concerning animal meridians occurs when the horse's hair stands on end in a line over the path of the bladder meridian. Several practitioners have reported seeing the pilomotor reaction within minutes of needle insertion. This example illustrates how a single acupoint, a specific point that corresponds to a known neural structure, can stimulate the entire meridian.

Claude Darras, a French medical doctor, has conducted fascinating experiments in an attempt to trace the physical effects of acupuncture and the pathways of meridians. When he injected a radioactive isotope into an acupuncture point, it did not follow an anatomical pathway but rather a path of specific, predictable meridians. Isotopes injected into nonacupuncture points did not exhibit this characteristic. Furthermore, when the isotope stopped moving, Darras restimulated its movement by needling the point directly beneath the injection site.

The meridians are abbreviated with a common numbering system adopted by the World Health Organization to allow a universal reference to each meridian.

MERIDIAN ABBREVIATIONS

LU Lung

LI Large Intestine

ST Stomach

SP Spleen

HT Heart

SI Small Intestine

BL Bladder

KI Kidney

PC Pericardium

TH Triple Heater

GB Gall Bladder

LIV Liver

GV Governing Vessel

CV Conception Vessel

THE PAIRED MERIDIANS

The anatomical course of each meridian is described. Each Yin meridian is matched with a corresponding Yang meridian. Each pair governs an associated tissue and sense organ. The associated tissues and sense organs can be helpful in the diagnosis of TCM patterns. For example, if a horse has a chronic problem with bowed tendons and damaged ligaments, the acupuncturist may diagnose and treat a disorder of the Liver because tendons are the associated tissue of the Liver meridian.

The alarm points and association points are also listed. Alarm points (*Mu* points) function as diagnostic tools. They are called alarm points because they react to palpation when internal organs are involved or energy is imbalanced as opposed to involvement of the meridian. They are usually located along various meridians on the ventral chest and abdomen directly above or near the related organ. Association points (*Shu* points) are used to transport Qi to the specific organ with which it is associated. They are valuable indicators to help identify which meridian is imbalanced. They are all located on the bladder meridian just to the side of the dorsal or top midline. They are important in the treatment of disorders in the organs or in the sense organs.

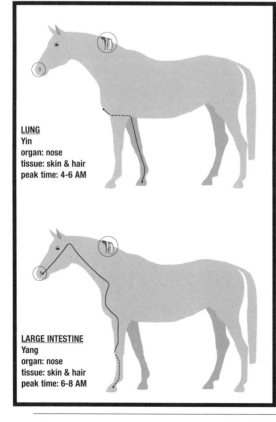

LUNG
Yin
organ: nose
tissue: skin & hair
peak time: 4-6 AM

LARGE INTESTINE
Yang
organ: nose
tissue: skin & hair
peak time: 6-8 AM

LUNG AND LARGE INTESTINE

The Lung meridian is a Yin meridian with 11 points. Beginning internally, it surfaces in the first space between the ribs over the pectoral muscles. This meridian travels down the horse's front limb on the inside and ends on the caudal medial coronary band. Its maximum energy flow is 4 a.m. to 6 a.m. The Lung meridian's associated tissue is skin and hair, while its sense organ is the nose. Dry environments adversely affect this meridian by drying the skin, nose, and lung. Its alarm point is LU1, and its association point is BL13. The Lung meridian is paired with the Large Intestine meridian and is used to treat and diagnose respiratory problems, skin diseases, and front leg lameness.

The Large Intestine meridian is a Yang meridian and contains 20 points. Starting on the craniomedial aspect of the coronary band, it travels up the inside of the forelimb to the carpus or knee. This meridian crosses laterally over the knee and up over the elbow and shoulder, across the neck and cheek to end on the opposite side just below the nostrils. Its peak energy is between 6 a.m. and 8 a.m. Paired with the Lung Meridian, it is also associated with the skin and hair. Its sense organ is the nose. The alarm point is ST25, and the association point is BL25. The Large Intestine meridian can be useful for diarrhea, colic, and front leg lameness.

THE STOMACH AND SPLEEN

The Stomach meridian is Yang and has 45 points along its path. It begins just below the eye and goes to the mouth then back on the ventral part of the neck, adjacent to the ventral midline to the groin. It continues down the front of the hind limb to end

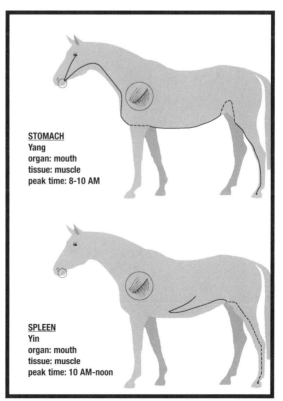

STOMACH
Yang
organ: mouth
tissue: muscle
peak time: 8-10 AM

SPLEEN
Yin
organ: mouth
tissue: muscle
peak time: 10 AM-noon

at the midline or just outside the midline of the coronary band of the hind foot. The Stomach meridian's peak time is 8 a.m. to 10 a.m. It is associated with muscles and uses the mouth as its sense organ. Its alarm point is C12, located midway between the xiphoid (base of the breastbone) and the umbilicus. The association point is BL21. It is paired with the Spleen meridian. The Stomach meridian is used in the treatment of gastrointestinal ulcers, colic, eye problems, and front leg lameness.

The Spleen meridian is Yin with 21 acupoints. It begins at the back inside of the coronary band of the hind foot and passes along the inside of the hind limb. The meridian then courses across the abdomen almost to the elbow where it turns back across the abdomen to end by the 10th intercostal (between the ribs) space at the level of the shoulder joint. Its peak energy time is 10 a.m. to 12 noon. Paired with the Stomach, it is also linked with muscles and the mouth. The alarm point is LIV13 and association point is BL20. The Spleen meridian is helpful in cases of tying up (exertional rhabdomyelosis), reproductive disorders, and lameness in the hind leg.

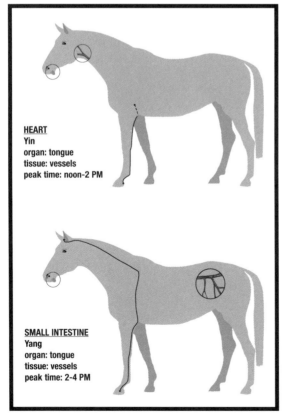

HEART
Yin
organ: tongue
tissue: vessels
peak time: noon-2 PM

SMALL INTESTINE
Yang
organ: tongue
tissue: vessels
peak time: 2-4 PM

THE HEART AND SMALL INTESTINE

The Heart meridian is a Yin meridian with nine points. It starts in the axilla or armpit and goes along the back of the forelimb and ends laterally on the caudolateral aspect of the coronary band. This meridian peaks between 12 noon and 2 p.m. and is associated with blood vessels and the tongue. Its alarm point is CV14, and the association point is BL15. It is paired with the Small Intestine meridian. The heart meridian is used for calming and for front leg lameness.

The Small Intestine meridian is a Yang channel and has 19 points. It begins on the lateral coronary band and courses up along the outside of the front limb. From there, it runs along the top of the neck to end adjacent to the front of the ear. It has its highest energy from 2 p.m. to 4 p.m. Since it is paired with the Heart meridian, it is associated with the vessels and the tongue. The alarm point for this meridian is CV4 and its association point is BL27. The Small Intestine meridian can be used for eye problems, colic, and front leg lameness.

THE BLADDER AND KIDNEY

The Bladder meridian is the most Yang meridian with 67 points. It begins at the corner at either side of the eye then travels back over the head and along the dorsal midline to the back of the scapula. At this point the meridian divides into two branches. Each branch continues caudally parallel along the midline, over the

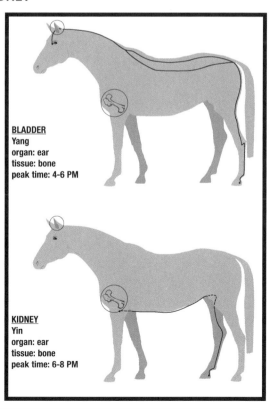

BLADDER
Yang
organ: ear
tissue: bone
peak time: 4-6 PM

KIDNEY
Yin
organ: ear
tissue: bone
peak time: 6-8 PM

hip, and down the back of the hind limb. The branches join just behind the stifle, and the meridian ends on the lateral heel. The Bladder meridian peaks from 4 p.m. to 6 p.m. Its associated tissue is bone, and its sense organ is the ear. The alarm point is CV3 and the association point is BL28. The Bladder meridian is paired with the Kidney meridian. It contains most of the association points for other meridians and is used diagnostically. If a horse is sensitive on the lung association point, the practitioner would check for pathology in the lung or on the pathway of the Lung meridian (the inside of the front leg). The Bladder meridian is also used for eye problems, neck pain, back pain, and hind limb lameness.

The Kidney meridian is Yin and contains 27 acupoints. It begins at a point between the bulbs of the heel of the hind foot, then travels along the inside of the hind limb and circles the medial malleolus or medial hock. It continues along the inside of the thigh and along the ventral abdomen next to the midline. It ends beside the sternum. The energy of the Kidney meridian is at its greatest from 6 p.m. to 8 p.m. Since it is paired with the Bladder, it is associated with bone and the ear. Its alarm point is GB25, and its association point is BL23. The Kidney meridian can be used for reproductive problems, urogenital diseases, lower back pain, and hock problems.

THE PERICARDIUM AND THE TRIPLE HEATER

The Pericardium meridian is Yin and is paired with the Triple Heater meridian. It has nine points and peaks between 8 p.m. and 10 p.m. It emerges superficially at a point inside the elbow and goes down the inside of the forelimb to the back of the knee. It drops straight down to end between the bulbs of the heel on the front foot. The Pericardium is similar to the Heart and the Small Intestine meridians in that its association tissue is vessels and its sense organ is the tongue. The alarm point for the Pericardium is CV17, and the association point is BL14. This meridian is affected in front leg lameness and emotional or behavioral problems.

The Triple Heater meridian is Yang and has 23 points. The term "Triple Heater" comes from the Chinese theory of three "burners" in the chest and abdomen. The first or Upper Burner is similar to a mist. It functions to distribute fluids all over the body. The second burner or the Middle Burner is like a maceration chamber. It is responsible for digestion and transportation of food and drink and their nourishment. The Lower Burner is like a ditch. It is responsible for the separation of the food into clean and dirty parts, and the excretion of the

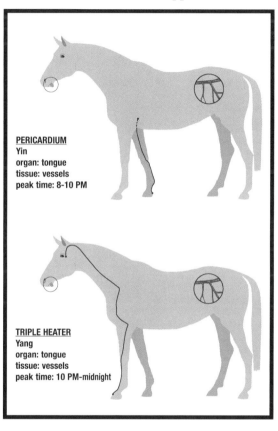

PERICARDIUM
Yin
organ: tongue
tissue: vessels
peak time: 8-10 PM

TRIPLE HEATER
Yang
organ: tongue
tissue: vessels
peak time: 10 PM-midnight

dirty parts. The Triple Heater meridian begins at the dorsal midline of the front foot at the coronary band and courses over the front of the leg to the shoulder. It then continues along the neck to the base of the ear and ends on the lateral orbit where the eyelash would be. The Triple Heater contains its highest energy between 10 p.m. and 12 midnight. It, too, is associated with the vessels and has the tongue for a sense organ. The alarm point is CV5, and the association point is BL22. The Triple Heater meridian can be used in ear and eye problems, neck pain, and front leg lameness.

THE GALL BLADDER AND LIVER

The Gall Bladder is a Yang meridian and has 44 acupoints. It begins just below the outside corner of the eye and travels to the inside of the ear. It crosses past the poll and along the neck to the scapula. The meridian then runs through the thorax to the abdomen and the end of the rib cage and travels on to the hip and down the outside of the hind limb. It ends on the outside of the coronary band. Its maximum energy is from 12 a.m. to 2 a.m. It has tissue association with tendons and its sense organ is the eye. The alarm point is GB24 and the association point is BL19. The Gall Bladder and the liver meridians,

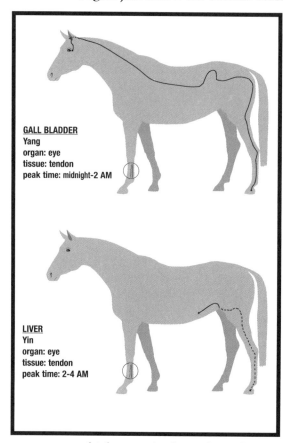

GALL BLADDER
Yang
organ: eye
tissue: tendon
peak time: midnight-2 AM

LIVER
Yin
organ: eye
tissue: tendon
peak time: 2-4 AM

which are paired, are the only meridians that have their alarm points on their own meridian pathways. The gall bladder meridian is sensitive in any musculoskeletal conditions including tendon problems, plus neck pain and eye disorders.

The Liver meridian is Yin and has 14 acupoints. It begins on the medial coronary band of the hind foot and follows the inside of the leg to the top and then heads to the end of the 17th rib. It ends at a point in the 13th intercostal space at the level of the elbow, which is also its alarm point (LIV14). The association point is BL18. Its highest energy level is between 2 a.m. and 4 a.m., and it is associated with hock and back problems, as well as tendons and the eye.

THE UNPAIRED MERIDIANS

The Governing Vessel meridian has 28 points and starts directly above the anus and below the tail head. It travels forward on the midline of the back, over the poll to a point between the upper lip and the upper gum. It is named "governing vessel" because it is on the most Yang aspect of the body and governs or gathers all Yang from the sun or environment. It is used in treating shock, apnea, and some bone conditions.

GOVERNING VESSEL

CONCEPTION VESSEL

The Conception Vessel meridian has 24 points and begins just below the anus. It continues forward along the ventral midline of the abdomen, thorax, neck, and head. It ends at a point on the midline ventral to the rim of the lower lip. This meridian is useful for reproductive disorders and for calming some horses.

CHAPTER 6

A Scientific Explanation of Acupuncture

Several scientific studies conducted over the past several years and more recent advances in the field of neuroscience are now providing a physiological basis for explaining how acupuncture works. Acupuncture repairs abnormally functioning tissues and organs by affecting the neurologic and endocrine systems. Acupuncture can affect the central and peripheral nervous systems to activate the body's endogenous or natural pain relief mechanisms. Acupuncture also stimulates the release of several neurotransmitters, chemical secretions that cause a desired reaction in another nerve, a muscle, or a gland. In the past, many people believed acupuncture was placebo; human patients only "thought" they were improving after acupuncture treatment. However, animals are unable to project their psyche onto a medical treatment. Thus, acupuncture's surprising effect on animals has negated the placebo theory.

Magnetic resonance imaging (MRI) measures neuronal activity and has helped to elucidate the effects of acupuncture. MRI has shown that stimulation of acupuncture points causes quantifiable changes in specific areas of the human brain. MRI also can demonstrate a central nervous system pathway for acupuncture by showing the areas of neural activity in response to acupuncture needling. Two acupuncture points, ST36 and LI4, have been shown to activate pathways in the brain involved in decreasing pain signals in the body.

Another study using functional MRI showed a relationship between acupoints for the treatment of eye disorders as suggested by ancient Asian literature and the corresponding brain localization for vision described by Western medicine. According to the study, acupuncture of a point related to vision on the lateral side of the foot would result in

AT A GLANCE

- Acupuncture can trigger the body's pain relief mechanisms.

- There are five theories about why acupuncture works. The most proven is that acupuncture stimulates increased blood supply, relieves local pain, and relaxes muscles.

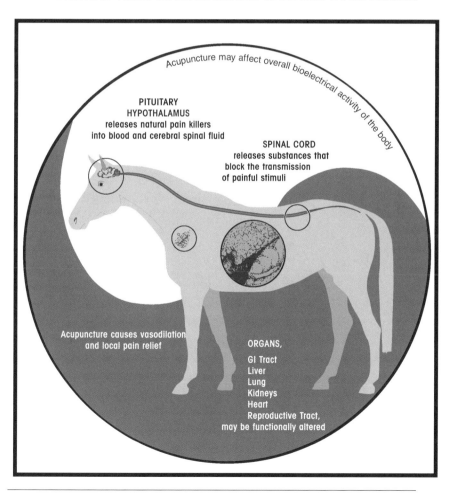

Acupuncture may affect overall bioelectrical activity of the body

PITUITARY
HYPOTHALAMUS
releases natural pain killers
into blood and cerebral spinal fluid

SPINAL CORD
releases substances that
block the transmission
of painful stimuli

Acupuncture causes vasodilation
and local pain relief

ORGANS,

GI Tract
Liver
Lung
Kidneys
Heart
Reproductive Tract,
may be functionally altered

activation of the occipital lobes of the brain, which control vision. Stimulation of the eye by a direct flashing light results in similar activation of the brain. Interestingly, acupuncture of other local areas only a few centimeters away from the vision-related acupoint resulted in no activation of the occipital cortex.

Acupuncture points correspond to four known neural structures. Acupuncture points lie directly over free nerve endings with blood vessels wrapped in connective tissue. Approximately 67 percent of the acupuncture points are Type I points or motor points. Motor points are areas near where the nerve enters into the muscle belly or middle of the muscle. These points produce maximum contraction of the associated muscle with minimal stimulation. Type II points are located on superficial nerves along the top of the back and midline of the belly. Type III points are located at highly dense points of outer nerves or network of nerves such as the lower leg. Type IV points are within tendons and correspond to Golgi/tendon organs. Golgi organs are named after an Italian neurologist, Camillo Golgi (1843-1926). A spindle-shaped sensory end organ or Golgi organ provides information about muscle tension to the brain. This structure allows you to stand upright without consciously contracting the muscles in your leg. These anatomical connections help in understanding how acupuncture uses the body's nervous system to achieve its effects.

There are five theories about how acupuncture works. In actuality, all five theories probably act together, with no single theory explaining all of acupuncture's effectiveness.

The first and oldest theory is referred to as the gate theory. Inhibitory neurons stop or "close the gate" on ascending fibers that carry information about pain. Therefore, signals are not able to reach the brain, and there is no perception of pain. An acupuncture stimulus is transmitted from the point to the central nervous system by afferent peripheral nerves, nerves that conduct impulses from the periphery of the body inward to the CNS. This is proven by injecting lidocaine into an acupoint. Lidocaine is a block similar to the injection a dentist gives before he or she would fill a cavity. It blocks the signal of pain to the brain. Similarly, the effect of acupuncture will be blocked because the signal is not able to reach the spinal cord.

Pain results from noxious stimuli applied to pain receptors in the skin, in the musculoskeletal system, or in visceral structures. Pain receptors are free nerve endings that transmit pain impulses or information regarding mechanical, chemical, or thermal stimuli. When the pain receptors are stimulated, nerve impulses are propagated along peripheral nerves to corresponding areas in the spinal cord. Some impulses are transmitted to several spinal segments above and below the point of entry of the painful stimulus to the spinal cord. The impulse also travels to the brain where pain is perceived.

There are two types of nerves that carry sensory information to the brain. C fibers are sensory receptors that carry information about pain, heat, and cold. C fibers are unmyelinated — not encased in a sheath of fatty material — and transmit information slower than A fibers. A fibers carry information regarding tension, contraction, and pressure, and they conduct impulses faster because they are large and myelinated. The myelin is a fatty material that acts as insulation for the nerve so that signals are not interrupted and are transmitted quickly. The theory is that when an acupoint is stimulated, the information travels through A fibers to the central nervous system. The information travels very fast and produces a lot of activity at the synapse or the point at which an impulse passes from one neuron to another. This abundance of activity at the synapse prevents other information from being transmitted to the brain. Therefore, the signal for pain perception is reduced or obliterated. Evidence shows that stimulation of acupuncture points can produce local pain relief. This theory, however, does not account for the delayed effects of acupuncture.

The next explanation of why acupuncture works is the most proven. Acupuncture stimulates increased blood supply, relieves local pain, and relaxes muscles. Studies have shown that in response to acupuncture, damaged cells will prompt a series of molecular events that result in activation of the protein bradykinin. Bradykinin is a powerful vasodilator and can increase the blood supply in the area. The additional blood brings more cells to the area to help repair tissues. Acupuncture also increases the immunity of local tissue by stimulating the large number of mast cells at each acupoint. These mast cells are a type of white blood cells that release histamine, another potent vasodilator. Histamine, in turn, will allow more blood to bring in more cells to fight infection. The fact that mast cells and nerve endings are in close proximity at an acupoint may be important in needling. These cell types are concentrated at all acupoints, and needling the point will quickly stimulate the cells to begin to repair damaged tissues.

The third theory is termed the humoral theory. "Humoral" pertains to elements or chemical substances in the blood that affect another nerve, muscle, or gland. When pressure is applied to an acupoint on the skin, sensory receptors such as pain, temperature, and pressure receptors are stimulated. Then afferent nerves bring the signal from the body's periphery to the central nervous system. The central nervous system then activates the hypothalamic-pituitary system at the base of the brain. The hypothalamic-pituitary gland releases neurotransmitters and natural pain-killing hormones that affect different body systems. For example, electroacupuncture has been shown to increase circulating levels of ACTH, adrenocorticotropic hormone, from the hypothalamic-pituitary system. ACTH goes through the bloodstream to the adrenal gland, triggering the release of cortisol, a natural steroid that reduces swelling and inflammation. Once released, the cortisol increases circulation, relieves muscle spasms, and stimulates related nerves and the body's defense system. Effects are seen on ovarian, testicular, thyroid, and parathyroid substances. Other chemicals produced by the body, including opioids, serotonin, and cholinergic and andrenergic compounds are released in addition to the cortisol. All of these substances are involved in the physiologic balance of the body. Endorphins (translated as endogenous + morphine) are also released from the hypothalamic-pituitary system in response to acupuncture. The endorphins can circulate in the blood for hours. All of these neurohormones can act at several different levels in the body to inhibit pain perception. Some endorphins are ten to one hundred times more potent than morphine.

The humoral theory is best shown by an experiment done in rats. Two rats were united surgically so that they shared blood. Acupuncture was performed on one rat, but the effects were seen in both rats. The result directly supports the theory that these neurohormones released into circulation are stimulated by acupuncture. This regulation of the pituitary-adrenal cortex system seems to encompass both stimulation and inhibition. The effect depends on the original state of the cerebral cortex at the time of treatment. Acupuncture has a homeostatic effect. If the body needs stimulation of neurohormones, acupuncture can initiate this. Conversely, if the body needs inhibition, acupuncture will initiate these processes.

Further proof that acupuncture works in part by releasing opiate-like substances is that acupuncture's analgesic effect is reversed with Naloxone®. Naloxone® is a medication that is a pure blocking agent at all known opioid receptors. Substances that block opioid biosynthesis will decrease the degree of acupuncture analgesia, and substances that inhibit degradation of opioids will prolong acupuncture analgesia. Opioids also will increase in concentration in the blood and the cerebral spinal fluid and decrease in brain areas during acupuncture analgesia. Certain mice that are genetically deficient in opioid receptors consistently have a poor response to acupuncture analgesia.

The lip twitch often used by horse people to restrain horses can be thought of as a form of acupuncture or acupressure. The plasma Beta-endorphin levels will double only five minutes after applying the twitch. The increase in Beta-endorphin correlates directly with the body's ability to tolerate pain. Opiate receptors are also present in the gastrointestinal tract and help regulate peristaltic activity. Beta-endorphin receptors are located on blood vessels and may contribute to the vessels' dilation seen with acupuncture.

The autonomic nervous system also can be stimulated with acupuncture. This is referred to as a viscerosomatic response and is the fourth theory explaining the effects of acupuncture. Needling certain points on the skin can exert impressive influences on internal organs such as the gastrointestinal tract and the reproductive tract. Neural impulses also may be transmitted through neuronal synapses in the spinal cord that stimulate nerves that regulate the activity of the internal organs. This may explain the bradycardia or decrease in heart rate associated with acupuncture.

Acupuncture may produce these effects by stimulating cyclic AMP, an enzyme leading to a release of different neurohormones from the adrenal gland. These hormones increase blood flow and reduce inflammation by washing out or removing accumulated waste products. The waste products may be the cause of some pain. This can sometimes be easily seen in people when heat and redness, or erythema, develop around the needle. The most common reported sensation reported after a needle has been inserted is a feeling of heat or warmth at the site. In horses the hair may stand on end after the needle has been inserted.

Finally, acupuncture channels are thought to be bioelectric. The channels allow transmission of nerve impulses due to the low electrical impedance. The electrical impedance can be easily measured at acupuncture points. This system has been described to work on a DC electronic signal that is produced and distributed by cells that support the transmission of a nerve signal. Stimulation of an acupuncture point acts to boost the DC signal being carried along the meridian. This is analogous to an electrical amplifier placed in a high-power tension wire; as the flow of energy through a meridian is weak or obstructed, the insertion of an acupuncture needle can "amplify" the energy and restore its flow.

Therefore, needles placed near the site of pain activate local mechanisms to reduce pain and promote healing. When needles are placed far away from the painful region, they activate the mid-brain and hypothalamic-pituitary axis to provide pain relief throughout the body via circulating neurohormones. Local and distal needling act synergistically to augment pain relief. As quality research continues, the interrelationship of these theories will be detailed. As modern research unravels the mysteries of acupuncture, there is a greater appreciation of the ancient Chinese and their philosophies of acupuncture.

CHAPTER 7

Different Modalities of Acupuncture

Acupuncture is not a quick fix. Inserting a few needles does not heal an injured horse or cure a disease. The horse usually shows some improvement with each treatment but generally requires several sessions. The frequency of acupuncture depends upon the problem and the method of treatment. More treatments are usually required for lingering problems.

The examining veterinary acupuncturist will first perform an acupuncture examination and determine the appropriate treatment points. A trained practitioner with knowledge of equine anatomy and a critical and accurate sense of touch can detect the points. Some practitioners use an electronic point finder that is simply an impedance meter. This instrument works because the skin at an acupoint has a lower level of electrical impedance or a higher level of con-

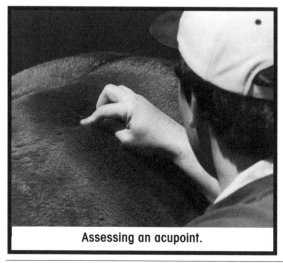

Assessing an acupoint.

ductivity. The practitioner runs the hand-held instrument over the horse's body, and a sound indicates where the point is located.

Two complications can arise from needling, but they rarely occur if done by a qualified acupuncturist. Acupuncture needles are very fine and usually very flexible, but a needle may break off under the skin from a series of strong muscle contractions. Hypodermic needles, which are used when injecting substances into an acupoint (aquapressure), are less forgiving and can break off instantly if the horse moves suddenly as the needle is inserted.

AT A GLANCE

• A veterinarian will perform an acupuncture examination before deciding what points to treat.

• Dry needling is the most traditional acupuncture technique. It involves the use of solid needles with a stainless steel shaft.

• Aquapuncture involves the injection of a substance, such as a vitamin, into an acupoint.

• Warm needling is called moxibustion and involves burning a Chinese herb on the needles or on the skin.

Infection is another possible complication. Specialized acupuncture needles are less likely to cause infection because they are not hollow. Hypodermic needles are more likely to carry foreign material on the skin into the acupoint. On the positive side, increased circulation and a high level of mast cells at acupuncture points may help to combat infection.

Acupuncture sometimes causes exaggerated relaxation. Some clients report that their horses are overly relaxed the following acupuncture treatment and want to rest or lie down more than normal. The horses usually improve over the next 24 hours. Acupuncture also may have different effects at different times of the day. Stimulation during a certain time of the day may increase levels of endorphins while stimulation at a different time of the day may decrease levels according to what is best for the patient.

Acupuncture treatments can be done several ways. Each modality has a different indication and limitation. Sometimes more than one acupuncture modality is used on a single horse to treat a problem or injury. Some acupuncturists prefer to use different modalities for certain cases, and some horses tolerate different modalities better. For example, some horses are very needle shy, especially in areas around their head. Laser acupuncture may be more suitable for these horses so they do not hurt themselves or the handlers during the therapy. The drawback is that only stimulate one point can be stimulated at a time and treatment takes longer. As mentioned in Chapter 4, there is certainly more than one way to treat a horse in Traditional Chinese Medicine. Also, if a certain method is not effective, another method may be tried.

DRY NEEDLING

The most common technique associated with acupuncture, dry needling is usually what most acupuncture practitioners use to treat horses. This is also referred to as "white needling" because no blood is involved.

The needles are solid and have a stainless steel shaft and a

copper or plastic handle. The needles are extremely fine and are difficult to insert without a thicker handle. Some needles have a sleeve or insertion tube that allows the user to tap them through the skin more easily. The needles are

Dry needling is the most common technique.

sterile, and practitioners should not reuse them. The needles are made in varying lengths and gauges, or diameters, for use in different locations of the body. For example, acupuncture needles are long and reach areas not typically accessible by other therapies. This allows for stimulation of more tissues and a more dramatic effect as compared to acupressure or

Tools of the Trade: acupuncture needles (1); a low-current electrical device (2); a laser (3); moxa, a Chinese herb used for warm needling (4); and vitamin B (5), which is injected into an acupoint.

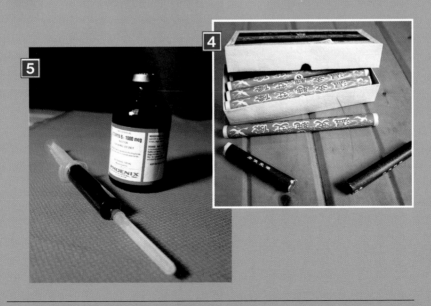

The acupuncture examination begins with a check of the tongue (1), then palpation of acupoints for reactivity (2-8).

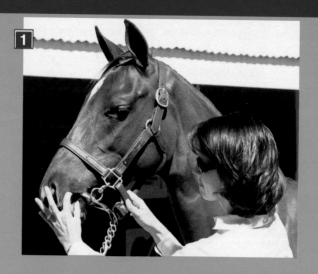

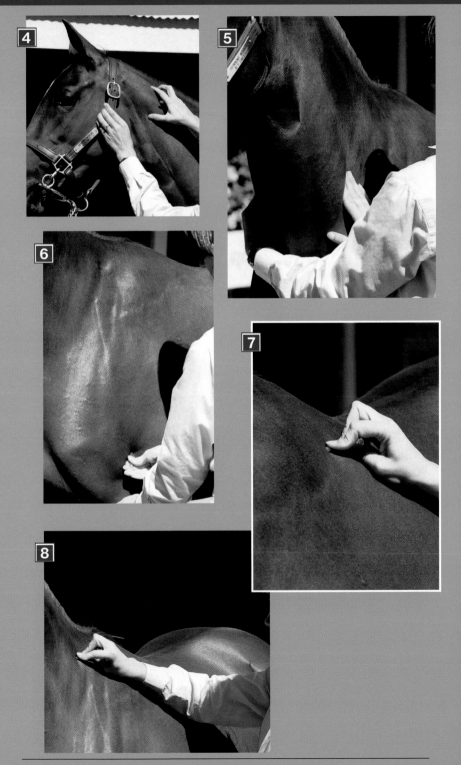

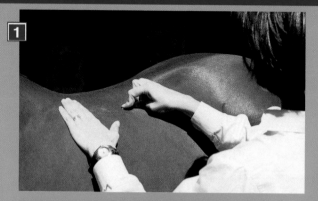

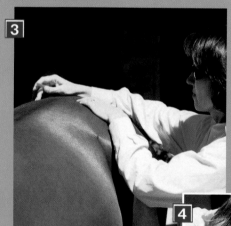

The diagnostic examination
— palpation of Association
points along the Bladder
meridian (1-4).

Photos 1-3: Palpation of the joints for heat, pain, and swelling after the area is localized by the diagnostic TCM examination; palpation of the soft tissue structures and the *Ting* points (4).

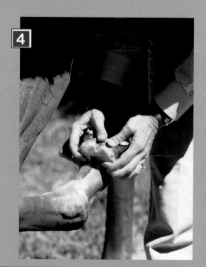

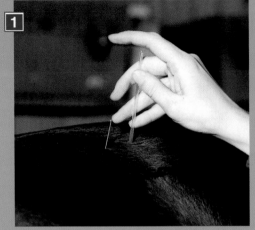

Tapping in a needle (1); connecting needles to a low-current electrical device (2); electroacupuncture (3) joins the needles with small wires and stimulates them with the device.

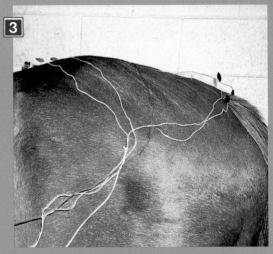

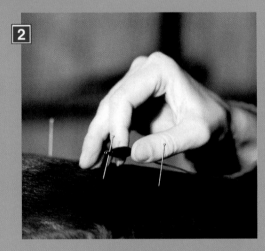

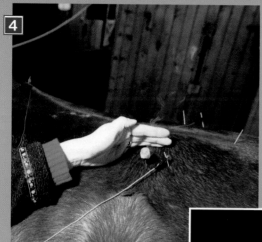

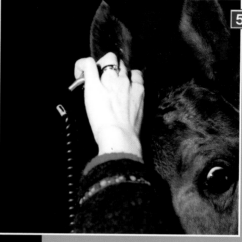

With moxibustion (4), a special herb is burned to heat the needle and stimulate the acupoint; low-power lasers can be used to stimulate acupoints (5); aquapuncture can stimulate an acupoint for a longer period (6).

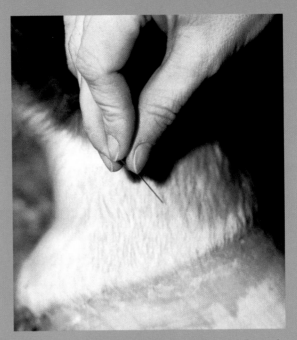

Ting points, located in the coronary band, are points of energy
interchange as well as of transference of energy. The quality of
blood can provide the acupuncturist
with crucial information.

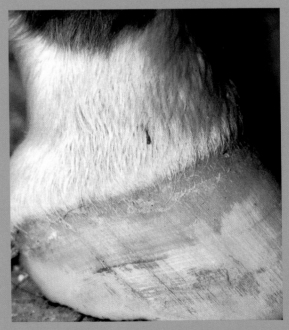

massage of the acupoints.

Acupuncture needles are placed in the appropriate tissues and left in place for 15 to 30 minutes, depending on the condition being treated. The acupuncturist may intermittently twirl or twist the needles to get the desired stimulation. Human pain clinics have shown that the manipulation of dry needles causes microscopic tissue injury, which creates an injury potential or electrical currents of injury. An injury potential is simply a small electrical current that is created when cells are damaged and their contents are dispersed. This is advantageous because the potential attracts white blood cells to the site of injury. The cells facilitate healing of the injured site.

AQUAPUNCTURE

Aquapuncture is using a hypodermic needle to inject substances into the acupoint. Usually a 25-gauge 1.5-inch hypodermic needle is used. Some examples of substances used for aquapuncture include saline, vitamins, DMSO, serapin, iodine, hormones, and medications. The injection creates pressure or mild irritation to the acupoint and may keep the point stimulated for a longer period of time than does dry needling. This technique is good for horses that do not tolerate leaving the needles in.

BLEEDING THE ACUPOINT

Another way to stimulate an acupoint is to make it bleed, a practice most often used in horses with laminitis. A larger hypodermic needle (14 to 16 gauge needle) pricks the point and makes it bleed. Laminitis is most commonly treated by bleeding the *Ting* points because the disease process involves stagnation of blood in the meridians of the front legs. Bleeding a *Ting* point allows the *Qi* in the meridian to flow more readily without the obstruction of blood at the point.

ACUPRESSURE

Another way to stimulate an acupoint is acupressure. Firm massage is applied to the specific point for 20 to 30 minutes. Acupressure offers horse owners a way to participate in the treatment of their horse. Owners can help by learning what to do for their horses between acupuncture treatments. Combining acupressure with acupuncture treatment will enhance healing and maintain health. Acupressure relaxes horses that are in heavy training and helps to relieve muscle spasms. Acupressure also makes the horse more receptive to acupuncture treatments because he is more accustomed to sensations at the acupoints.

CUPPING

Cupping is a technique that combines creating a vacuum and thermotherapy. It is more commonly used in human patients because the horse's coat makes it difficult to create a vacuum. This ancient Chinese technique involves applying negative pressure to acupuncture points. A small, globular glass cup is coated with cotton and alcohol and the interior of the cup is ignited. The cup is then firmly placed over the acupoint. Fire consumes the oxygen in the cup, creating a vacuum. This causes the skin and underlying tissues to be pulled up into the cup, causing irritation of the acupoint. The heat used to create a vacuum does not give off enough heat to burn the skin.

WARM NEEDLING

Warm needling is called moxibustion and involves burning a Chinese herb, mugwart or *Artemisia vulgaris*, on the needles or on the skin. The herb, the only one used for moxibustion, is rolled into a cylinder similar to a cigar; then a one-centimeter section is cut and put on the needle. When the acupuncturist ignites the cylinder of herb, it produces heavy smoke. Burning the herb is used to heat the acupuncture needle and thereby stimulate the acupoint. Moxibustion is good for the treatment of arthritis and other chronic pain. In TCM, arthritis and chronic pain are thought to be related to Cold within the meridian. The needle is used to carry heat into deeper tissues and to the affected meridian. Moxibustion should not be used in cases of acute inflammation or infec-

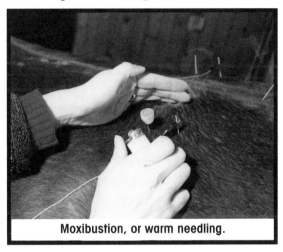

Moxibustion, or warm needling.

tious disease. In TCM, these diseases are thought to be associated with Heat. Therefore it is contraindicated to apply heat to the acupoint.

In Traditional Chinese Medicine, warm needling is thought to open meridian flow and strengthen Yang. Laboratory animals with inflammatory granulomas (a chronic, nodular skin tumor) on their backs were treated with moxibustion. After eight days of treatment, effusion, or drainage, from the sacs had half the volume of effusion compared to that non-treated animals. Moxibustion enhances the immune system by promoting complement, which is a substance or protein in the blood that helps combat infection.

ELECTROACUPUNCTURE

Electroacupuncture joins the needles with small wires and stimulates them with a low-current electrical device. The device may be attached directly to the handle of the needle or to damp sponges applied to the needle. This method is a variation of transcutaneous electrical neural stimulation or TENS therapy. TENS therapy is the use of electrode patches applied to the skin to stimulate nerves. It is commonly used by physical therapists for rehabilitation of joint injuries. The effects of electroacupuncture are longer lasting than those of dry needling or TENS therapy. The intensity of the electrical current is adjusted to a level just below discomfort and increased every five minutes, as the horse becomes tolerant. Acute processes require a shorter treatment time of approximately 10 to 15 minutes. Chronic conditions will require 20 to 30 minutes of stimulation for the best results.

Electroacupuncture causes changes in the morphological characteristics and alignment of collagen fibers as can be seen by a microscope. Treatment with electroacupuncture causes the collagen fibers to align better and have more tensile strength. In turn, this makes the tendons and ligaments made of collagen fibers less susceptible to injury. Therefore, there are important implications for both orthopedic and soft tissue diseases to facilitate healing of bones, tendons, and ligaments and reduce the pain associated with those injuries.

Electroacupuncture is much stronger than manual manipulation of dry needles. It is, therefore, used to achieve acupuncture analgesia, which is pain control during surgical procedures. Electroacupuncture also is used to promote wound healing, decrease tissue swelling, and produce strong muscular contractions. The latter may be advantageous for strength, endurance, and velocity training; preventing and loosening adhesions after an injury; reduction of muscle spasms; increasing the blood supply; promoting lymphatic draining; and facilitating muscle contractions in muscles with damaged nerves. Electroacupuncture should not be applied over the lower back or abdomen of a pregnant mare. It can be used on other locations on pregnant mares with caution. It also should not be applied over cancerous areas, over the eyes, for undiagnosed pain, or transcerebrally (across the skull).

LASER

Low-power lasers also can be used to stimulate acupoints. Laser is a very useful tool for horses that are needle shy or for points that are in difficult or dangerous locations. Horse have strong subcutaneous muscles and, therefore, a very strong skin twitch that makes it hard to maintain the needle at a particular site such as the flank area. Lasers may be useful in these cases. Ultrasound machines also can be used to stimulate an acupoint. These techniques are noninvasive and simple to perform.

IMPLANTS

Implants also may be used in acupoints to get a longer-lasting effect. Implants may be gold wire, gold BBs, stainless steel wire, cat gut, or surgical staples. Implantation causes severe localized inflammation and prolonged stimulation of the acupoint. The implants are inserted through a large sterile needle. They are left there indefinitely. They are ideal for chronic conditions because the acupuncture stimulation is constant and repetitive treatments are not necessary.

PNEUMOACUPUNCTURE

Pneumoacupuncture is the injection of air into the acupoint. This is most commonly used for shoulder injuries or radial nerve paralysis. The treatment involves the introduction of air into these injuries to bring oxygen to the damaged nerves and help them heal.

In conclusion, acupuncture may involve one or several instruments and methods. The modality that is used depends on the horse's diagnostic acupuncture examination and the problem. Different modalities are advantageous for certain locations and conditions.

CHAPTER 8
Acupuncture as a Diagnostic Tool

A Traditional Chinese Medicine examination can be used to help diagnose conditions in the horse. Some veterinarians use sensitivity at acupuncture points to localize a problem, then they treat the problem with Western methods. If your horse has a problem that you think might benefit from acupuncture, you should consult with your veterinarian or a certified acupuncturist in your area.

TRADITIONAL CHINESE MEDICINE EXAMINATION

Traditional Chinese Medicine practitioners' observations of patients differ from those of an conventional Western medicine practitioner. A Traditional Chinese Medicine examination notes subtle changes.

Energy or *Qi* in the body circulates every 24 hours. Blocked energy indicates the presence of a problem. Obstructions in *Qi* result in pain at certain points along the pathway or at Association points for that meridian. Pain at an acupoint is detected by applying moderate pressure at the acupoint. A sensitive Association point indicates trouble along the associated meridian. If both the Association point and the Alarm point are sensitive, there is an organ problem. If the Association point is sensitive but not the Alarm point, there is a problem along the meridian or channel.

The following example illustrates this diagnostic method. An acupuncture practitioner examines the Association points on a horse and finds the Stomach Association point is sensitive to deep palpation. The horse reacts by pulling away and pinning his ears when the practitioner applies manual pressure to the Stomach Association point. The practitioner then palpates the Alarm point for the Stomach to check for organ involvement. The horse has no sensitivity or reaction when pressure is applied to the Stomach Alarm point, so the practitioner looks on the inside of the hind leg along the course of the Stomach meridian. There is local pain when the practitioner palpates the points close to the stifle. The problem is then localized to the inside of the stifle.

> ## AT A GLANCE
>
> • A Traditional Chinese Medicine exam can be an important diagnostic tool.
>
> • Palpation of painful acupoints or a combination of points can help locate a problem.
>
> • Sensitivity to acupressure varies from horse to horse.
>
> • Many diagnostic points lie on the Bladder meridian, which runs alongside the vertebral column where spinal nerves emerge at the head of each intercostal space.

Therefore, information gained from the acupuncture exam can help decide what area to palpate, flex, or radiograph. The TCM examination is a diagnostic tool that can be used to its fullest potential in conjunction with a thorough Western physical examination. In the example above, the practitioner would then block, ultrasound, radiograph, and possibly treat the inside of the stifle to complete the examination.

A TCM examination can give a more complete picture of the problem. Personality or the horse's behavior, pulse qualities, and the appearance of the tongue also can be used in the diagnosis. For instance, some horses' personalities are related to specific TCM diseases. The temperamental chestnut Thoroughbred filly is said to be a Fire constitution. She is more prone to pathology in the Heart and Small Intestine meridians. Conversely, the palomino Quarter Horse gelding is more Earth constitution. He is more prone to Stomach and Spleen meridian problems. A certified practitioner will palpate acupoints and determine the horse's reaction. The central nervous system reflects a map of pain based on the meridians or channels. When pain is present, inflammation, an increase or decrease in circulation, and increased or decreased muscle tone also are present. Therefore, when the meridians are palpated, the examiner will notice a difference in the reflexes and a difference in the quality of tissue. The practitioner applies a light, consistent pressure from point to point and notes the reaction.

If there is obstruction, the point is very reactive. The acupoints may be firm, yielding to pressure, tightening under pressure, warm, cold, etc. A reactive point might trigger a muscle spasm or an evasive or aggressive reaction. Some horses will feel so much pain when pressure is applied to a

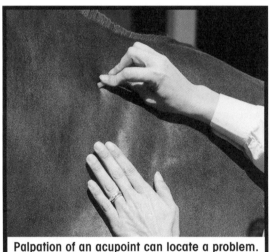

Palpation of an acupoint can locate a problem.

point that they will bite or kick. Generally, a reaction to light pressure indicates a more acute condition, and response to deep pressure indicates a long-standing condition.

Palpation of painful acupoints or a combination of points can help locate a problem. The acupuncturist can then translate the map and determine the source of the pain. Groups of points can indicate a problem in the stifle, in the hock, or elsewhere, or the presence of an internal disease. A single point cannot be used for diagnosis. If one point is sensitive, other points must be checked to see if the pain can be further localized.

Diagnostic acupuncture should be used with other modalities, including nerve blocks, flexion tests, ultrasound, radiology, and nuclear scintigraphy to achieve the best diagnosis and the best possible treatment.

Horses have different degrees of sensitivity. Therefore, detecting sensitive acupoints properly takes years of practice. Sensitivity to acupuncture can differ among breeds and within breeds just as those horses react differently to other stimuli. Similarly, young foals have different responses than older horses. Diagnostic acupuncture is very difficult in horses that are being treated with corticosteroids because acupoints are less reactive. The corticosteroids block the inflammation that makes acupoints reactive. As a result, the practitioner might obtain false information. Horses with acute diseases also are difficult to palpate. After an injury, there may be reduced reactivity for three to four days. It is not known why this occurs.

Many of the acupoints used for diagnostic purposes are to the outside of the dorsal midline between the long muscles of the back. Some of these points relate to systemic physiology, local physiology, local anatomy, or endocrinology. Superficial pain felt in organic disease usually occurs where sensory nerves and segmental nerves from the viscera enter the spinal cord. Many diagnostic points lie on the Bladder meridian. This meridian runs alongside the vertebral column where spinal nerves emerge at the head of each intercostal space.

Some very skilled acupuncturists can use *Ting* points, the points around the coronary band, for diagnosis. This is done by feeling each *Ting* point to see if the point is hard, soft, firm, fluidy, hot, or cold. The meridian related to the abnormal *Ting* point is then examined.

Trigger points also can be incorporated in the diagnostic examination. They are only present when there is injury or disease; they don't show up in healthy subjects. Trigger points are usually tender to pressure only when pathologic changes occur in related musculoskeletal structures. Direct trauma, acute myositis (inflammation in the muscle), chronic muscular strain, arthritis, nerve injuries, and neuromuscular disorders can initiate trigger points. With an injury, constant irritation continually bombards the central nervous system with afferent, or painful, stimuli. This bombardment creates abnormal activity in the centers of the spinal cord that process painful stimuli. This, in turn, leads to responses in muscles away from the injured area. People who experience arthritis can relate to this because a painful trigger point in their neck or back will hurt when the arthritis in their hands is particularly bad. The sensitive trigger point acts as a new afferent stimulus, or stimuli that go to the spinal cord and brain in addition to the stimuli from the injured area. Therefore, if one blocks the trigger point, the cycle is terminated and the pain ceases.

Commercial instruments can help the practitioner locate these painful trigger points. Most of the instruments available measure the electrical conductivity at each point and may help for some novice veterinarians. These instruments work on the premise that injury causes a change in the electrical current as a result charged ions leaking across the damaged cell membrane. If the area over the shoulder normally has an electrical current of 1, the current after an injury may be 10 due to the rupture of cells and the change in composition of the tissues. This current of injury is the reason some species are able to regenerate limbs; amphibians "grow" a new appendage when the leg is removed because the damaged cells have a higher electrical current. This stimulates cells to replicate and replace the lost leg. Mammals do not have this ability but they do have a local change in the electrical current that helps speed healing when there is an injury.

Dr. Oswald Kothbauer, a dairy cow vet from Austria, best illustrates how TCM can be used as a diagnostic tool. Using Western methods, he would diagnose sick cows. He then went over their bodies with his hands, looking for painful points. He developed the ability to predict where points would appear in relation to certain specific diseases. He then took normal cows and irritated their organs to see where they would become sensitive. When he irritated a cow's uterus with iodine, a painful point would appear on the surface of the skin. This point corresponded to an acupoint specific for the uterus. It appeared at the same site for all the cows. In those cows with white hair, he reported that the area was red and the hair would stand up. The electrical resistance at the area also would decrease as measured by an ohmmeter.

In another example, an equine veterinarian successfully used a TCM examination to pinpoint fetlock pain in 327 racehorses. He used a thorough TCM diagnostic exam to evaluate each horse. The points specific for fetlock pain were sensitive in every horse. The sensitive points disappeared after the suspicious fetlock joint was blocked with an intra-articular joint block. The blocks eliminate the pain in the joint and, therefore, eliminate the sensitivity in the acupoint.

Lameness of the equine foot that involved purely extra-articular structures such as abscesses was not associated with channel imbalance or sensitivity to pressure at the acupoints. Therefore, certain problems such as an abscess in the

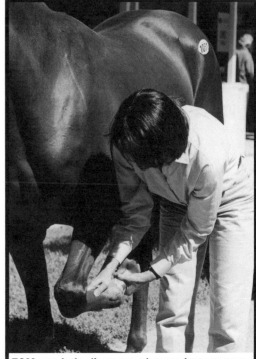

TCM can help diagnose obscure lamenesses.

foot cannot always be diagnosed with TCM. However, conditions associated with intra-articular inflammation were reflected by sensitive acupoints in the TCM examination. Furthermore, horses with joint inflammation but no lameness could be confirmed by the intra-articular anesthesia. When the horses' joints were blocked, normal responses to pressure were re-established and the acupoints palpated normally.

TCM can play a key role in diagnosis of obscure lameness by identifying syndromes through patterns of sensitivity at certain points. A group of points that are sensitive in the diagnostic examination may indicate hock pain or foot pain, and so on. If a group of body points is sore on palpation, a predictable anatomical area is involved and is usually the source of the soreness. This can be used in conjunction with conventional diagnostics to find the source of lameness. It is especially helpful in hindquarter lameness. It is worth noting that healthy horses do not have sensitive acupoints.

TYPICAL TCM EXAMINATION

A typical TCM examination that I would perform on a horse is as follows:

1) I stroke the horse's neck and get him/her to relax, while assessing the pulse under the jaw.

2) I ask the owner pertinent medical history questions both related to the presenting complaint and related to the Five Phase Theory or the Eight Element Theory. The questions concerning the history will depend on the disease process.

3) I ask what Western medicine diagnostic procedures have been done and the results of those procedures. If I localize a problem to an area that has not been blocked, radiographed, or further explored, I recommend those tests be done.

4) I palpate acupoints along the neck, back, and hindquarters looking for sensitivity or reaction at those points. If sensitivity is found at a particular point, I check related points for

sensitivity. For example, if I suspect pain from the hock area in a horse that does not want to jump, I double check other hock points to try to make all the pieces of the puzzle fit together.

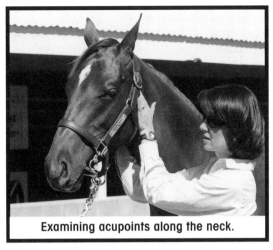

Examining acupoints along the neck.

5) I select a treatment protocol and a schedule of treatment sessions. I go over what type of response the owner can expect and try to relate the TCM diagnosis with the Western diagnosis.

CHAPTER 9
Acupuncture for Specific Conditions

A cupuncture can be used for treatment of almost every disease that occurs in horses. However, Western medicine probably would be the treatment of choice for certain advanced conditions, such as using penicillin to treat a lung infection. As research evolves, we will better understand what diseases can be treated more efficiently with acupuncture versus Western medicine or with both. No one form of medicine has all the answers. Therefore, the creative veterinarian can integrate the best Western medicine, acupuncture, physical therapy, and prevention to provide the optimal therapeutic plan. Acupuncture can be an alternative therapy for seemingly hopeless cases that have been unresponsive to conventional therapy or a primary treatment for appropriate conditions. In my experience, for example, horses with sore backs respond more quickly to acupuncture than they do to more conventional treatment.

Most horse ailments are extremely receptive to acupuncture treatment. The number of treatments required depends on the type and duration of the condition. In the author's experience, the longer the problem has existed, the greater the number of acupuncture treatments required to see improvement. The duration of the effectiveness varies from a few hours to years, depending on the problem. Acupuncture should never be used to replace good management. The horse should be properly shod, and the saddle should fit correctly. A veterinarian should see the horse regularly and provide preventative care such as deworming, vaccinating, dental examinations, and a general physical examination.

The goal of acupuncture therapy is to stimulate and strengthen the body's adaptive and homeostatic mechanisms. A horse in training endures stress to its musculoskeletal system. Acupuncture sets up a process for tissue healing by removing toxins from the body and increasing the blood flow. It also can release natural cortisone to reduce swelling and relieve pain, which can interfere with the animal's daily activities. Acupuncture can help build the body's immune system and enhance a horse's health.

> ## AT A GLANCE
>
> • Acupuncture can be used to treat nearly every equine disease or condition.
>
> • In lame horses, acupuncture will relieve muscle tension and pain and facilitate healing.
>
> • Most back problems respond very well to acupuncture.
>
> • Acupuncture has been used successfully to treat fertility and libido problems.

Animals in athletic training can benefit from regular and preventative acupuncture. Some Thoroughbred racehorses receive regular treatments, as do show jumpers, dressage horses, and other competitors. The frequency depends on the level and intensity of training. Another advantage of acupuncture is that the patient may not be able to receive medications, either systemic or local, due to medication regulations in each sporting discipline.

LAMENESS

Lameness is a significant problem for athletic horses. Because the horse has such a large muscle mass, lameness or pain in one limb can lead to severe muscle cramping as a result of the altered gait. Acupuncture will relieve the muscle tension and pain and facilitate healing of the injury. It is used to treat such lameness-causing conditions as navicular syndrome, sidebone, ringbone, laminitis, bone spavin, and all types of degenerative joint disease. The results vary and depend on the disease process and the individual. As mentioned previously, chronic problems requires more treatments before improvement is seen. The aforementioned conditions as well as neck pain, short stepping, dragging one toe, and stumbling can and will respond to acupuncture.

BACK PROBLEMS

The diagnosis and treatment of back pain with acupuncture were first documented in detail in the ancient Chinese veterinary text, *Yuan-Heng Liao MaJi* (*Yuan-Heng's Therapeutic Treatise of Horses*) published 385 years ago. Back pain, a common and serious problem in sport horses, responds extremely well to acupuncture. These horses usually require six to nine treatments and should remain in training while they are being treated. There is usually marked improvement after three to five treatments. After this initial series, horses need minimal treatment. Chronic back pain can be related to soft-tissue inflammation, myofascial pain, musculotendinous injuries, or ligamentous problems. Myofascial pain refers to pain that originates from swollen muscles contained within fasciae. The fascia does not stretch and the pressure within the bundle is painful. Musculotendinous injuries are tears in the tendon fibers at the location where they adjoin the muscles. There are small tendons and ligaments that attach at every vertebra. Therefore, there are numerous potential locations for tears and pulls.

Fibromyalgia is another cause of back pain, and occurs when the muscle fibers become fibrotic and lose their elasticity. The patient experiences pain due to the recurrent and chronic muscle contractions. This physical strain can result from improper shoeing, poor equitation, poor saddle fit, overuse, or improper training.

Acupuncture cannot help back problems caused by a poorly fitting saddle. In one particular study of back pain, almost 90 percent of the horses had poorly fitting saddles.

Although these horses improve when the saddle is fitted properly, there can be residual damage to the ligaments and tendons that can benefit from acupuncture.

Spondylosis, or arthritis of the spinal column, is characterized by bony alterations in the vertebral body and intervertebral disc spaces leading to painful fusion of adjacent vertebral bodies. Inflammation in the surrounding structures leads to damage to the nerve roots as they exit the spinal cord. This results in pain and malfunctioning of the nerve's signal. Thermography of the lumbar and croup areas in these horses shows areas of lowered skin temperature due to alterations in blood flow. The goal of acupuncture in any form of arthritis, including spondylosis, is to relax the local muscles and the paraspinal muscles. This, in turn, should alleviate the tension of the intervertebral joints and reduce the inflammation of the joint between each vertebra.

The channels used to treat back pain are the Governing Vessel and the inner and outer Bladder channels. Dry needles, electroacupuncture, lasers, moxibustion, and aquapuncture are all useful for the treatment of back pain.

Acupuncture can be particularly useful for secondary compensatory problems associated with chronic or low-grade lameness. In human medicine musculoskeletal pain is accompanied by muscle shortening in the peripheral and paraspinal muscles from spasms and contractions. Secondary trigger points emerge and can be distant to the primary problem. Acupuncture breaks the cycle of abnormal reflex muscle contraction that can be associated with joint dysfunction by blocking the sensation of pain in the brain and releasing the body's own natural pain killers.

GASTROINTESTINAL DISEASE

Gastrointestinal diseases such as non-surgical colic, ulcers, inappetence (lack of appetite), and chronic diarrhea have all been successfully treated with acupuncture. A study on 100 rabbits and 45 humans reported that acupuncture has an effect on post-operative gastrointestinal atony, a lack of normal tone or movement of the gastrointestinal tract. Gastrointestinal atony is a detrimental side effect of abdominal surgery, such as colic surgery, in animals and especially in the horse. Stimulation with acupuncture needles of acupoint ST36, located on the front of the gaskin on the horse's hind leg, increased intestinal motility by increasing the number of intestinal contractions per minute and increasing the strength of contractions.

In human patients acupuncture relieved abdominal distention and pain. These patients defecated within twenty-four hours after surgery compared with seventy-two hours in patients that were not treated with acupuncture.

In addition, in an animal model of gut atony, acupuncture hastened the return of intestinal motility in rabbits that had had their vagal nerve transected, or cut in two. The vagus nerve innervates the gastrointestinal tract and stimulates peristalsis. When this nerve is cut, the motility of the gut is dramatically reduced. Acupuncture can restore gut motility within twenty-four hours.

It has also been observed radiographically that acupuncture can stimulate small intestinal motility. Animals were given a dye in their food that showed up radiographically. The dye was then followed as it moved through the gastrointestinal tract. The group that was treated with acupuncture was compared with the control group. Acupuncture not only increased peristaltic noises recorded with a stethoscope, but also increased intestinal emptying as seen on the radiographs.

In another report, 64 percent of horses that had gastrointestinal signs of colic related to cribbing responded to acupuncture treatment. Cribbing is usually associated with swallowing air and possibly wood or plastic. Horses that crib often have signs of colic. It is thought the colic is caused by gas distension after swallowing large quantities of air. Acupuncture may improve gastrointestinal motility so that the gas passes and the abdominal pain ceases.

Acupuncture for gastric ulcers has been studied and written about extensively. Acupuncture can help patients with gastrointestinal ulcers by opening the pylorus, the opening of the stomach to the rest of the intestines. Acupuncture accelerates the emptying of stomach contents. This works by stimulating a viscerosomatic response and causing increased peristaltic movement of the intestines. Needling also plays a role in regulatory secretion of gastric juice. Acupuncture reduces the amount of acid in the stomach in two ways. The contents of the stomach are emptied to the small intestine faster so there is less time for gastric acid to build up. Secondly, the cells that produce gastric acid in response to a meal are somewhat inhibited so there is less production of acid. Gastric hydrochloric acid production was one quarter the level in an acupuncture-treated group compared with a control group. Acupuncture of ST36 restores acidity, pepsin, and rennin in the stomach.

The effectiveness of acupuncture in relieving bile stones, diarrhea, and abdominal pain as well as in preventing post-colic operational side effects also has been studied and shown to work. Some practitioners think that horses that have had surgery for colic benefit from post-op acupuncture and have fewer side effects, i.e., ileus (reduced intestinal motility), lack of appetite, not passing manure, incisional edema, and edema around the sheath.

One extremely good study shows the benefits of acupuncture for diarrhea in pigs. In an experimental model, young pigs were induced with an enteropathogenic *E.coli* diarrhea. The pigs were divided into three treatment groups and a control group. The first group was treated with antibiotics. The second group was treated with dry acupuncture needles. The third group was treated with electroacupuncture. The survival rate of the pigs treated with dry needles was better than that of those treated with antibiotics specific for the *E.coli* and better than the untreated control group. Those treated with electroacupuncture, however, did worse.

The electroacupuncture was thought to have increased gastrointestinal motility too aggressively.

BEHAVIOR

Behavior problems may respond to acupuncture because the bad behavior may be caused by pain. These "behavior problems" may present as pinning the ears, switching the tail, kicking, being difficult to groom, rearing or bucking when a rider is trying to mount, refusing fences, or excessive and difficult estrus in mares. TCM can help to localize a source of pain, and the acupuncture can work to relieve the pain. Acupuncture also may help these horses by eliciting a sedative effect.

EXERTIONAL RHABDOMYOLYSIS

Exertional rhabdomyolysis is a disease in which the horse's muscles cramp severely either during or just after exercise. It is also referred to as tying up, Monday morning sickness, or azoturia. Fillies and mares are much more likely to get this condition than are colts, geldings, and stallions. There are varying degrees of the condition, and some horses will tie up repeatedly. Acupuncture helps this problem by encouraging muscle relaxation and natural cortisol release to alleviate the pain associated with muscle cramps. Acupuncture also facilitates healing of these muscles by increasing blood flow. Acute cases of tying up will get extraordinary relief from acupuncture. Chronic cases respond well but need to be treated frequently.

RESPIRATORY DISEASE

Respiratory diseases, including sinusitis, pharyngitis, chronic obstructive pulmonary disease (heaves), exercise-induced pulmonary hemorrhage (bleeders), and pneumonia, can all be helped with acupuncture. Infectious respiratory diseases may benefit from stimulation of some of the acupoints used for immune stimulation. Experimental research has clearly shown that acupuncture has the ability to reduce fever, increase antibody production, and increase the body's resistance to inflammation. Acupuncture for guarding against infection is derived from its influence on the breakdown of disease-causing agents by leukocytes (white blood cells) and on the production of antibodies to fight disease. Needling of ST36 can increase white blood cells, while stimulation of a sham acupoint will not cause an increase in white blood cells. A sham acupoint is a point that is not described by any text and not associated with a meridian. Acupuncture in asthma patients can increase breathing capacity up to 20 percent if those subjects are in good health otherwise.

INFERTILITY

Reproductive disorders in both stallions and mares respond well to acupuncture therapy, which will improve the overall health of the horse and thereby improve reproductive function. In the mare, there are protocols for irregular estrous cycles, metritis, vaginitis, pyometra, retained placenta, urine pooling, uterine inertia (lack of uterine tone or contractions), prevention of abortion, uterine and post-partum hemorrhage, prolapsed uterus, and insufficient lactation. A stallion may become reluctant to breed or lose libido if his back or legs hurt. In the stallion there are acupuncture therapies for lack of libido, orchitis (inflammation of the testis), paraphimosis (penile paralysis or inability to retract the penis in the sheath), and cryptorchidism (undescended or abdominal testis).

A retrospective study on the use of acupuncture to reduce the amount of uterine fluid in Thoroughbred mares was done in Central Kentucky. Rectal ultrasonography showed that acupuncture decreased the amount of uterine fluid approximately 24 hours after the treatment. The mares treated were all considered "problem" mares; they had been to the breeding shed an average of four times during the season, an unusually high number of times. The group of mares had been barren due to infertility an average of 2.8 years prior to the year they were treated with acupuncture. Again this figure is higher than average for broodmares. The overall pregnancy rate of the treated mares was 86 percent. The protocol included a minimum of two acupuncture treatments, one treatment before breeding and one treatment after breeding. The mares were all also treated with conventional medicine at the time of acupuncture treatment to include oxytocin, intrauterine antibiotics, and occasionally systemic antibiotics. Studies are under way to evaluate uterine clearance more objectively by measuring the pressure in the uterus following acupuncture treatment.

Aquapuncture also can be useful in treating infertility problems. This involves the injection of therapeutic substances directly into the acupoints. The use of prostaglandin in the acupoint termed *Bai Wei* has been used to stimulate luteolysis or disruption of the corpus luteum, triggering the mare to come back into heat. *Bai Wei* is located at the lumbosacral junction on the dorsal midline of the horse. A significantly smaller dose of prostaglandin can be used if it is injected into the acupuncture point as compared to conventional intramuscular injections. Similarly, hormones can be injected into acupoints to stimulate mares to cycle more normally.

RENAL DISEASE

Nephritis and cystitis also have been responsive to acupuncture treatment. These diseases may respond best if the therapy includes herbal remedies in addition to regular acupuncture treatment. The author has successfully used acupuncture and herbs for the treatment of post-foaling bladder paralysis. This occurs due to trauma to the nerves that supply the bladder during foaling.

DERMATOLOGICAL PROBLEMS

Skin diseases are usually caused by some type of allergic or infectious agent, namely external parasites. The cause must be eliminated before positive results can be achieved. In these cases acupuncture can help modulate the immune system and help the horse to overcome the problem. Points distal to the affected area may have to be used if the local area is too inflamed to insert an acupuncture needle safely.

TRAUMA

Trauma usually leads to severe bruising, broken bones, tearing of tendons and ligaments, lacerations of the skin, and nerve damage. Broken bones, hemorrhage, wounds, and lacerations must be tended to immediately, usually by conventional methods. Two aspects where acupuncture can greatly benefit the trauma patient are with bruising and soft tissue tears and with nerve damage. Acupuncture can relieve muscle soreness associated with trauma. It facilitates healing of bruises and soft tissue tears by increasing the blood flow and reducing the pain, thus allowing the animal to move more freely. This, in turn, prevents adhesions and scarring of the soft tissue structures.

Nerve damage responds because acupuncture can stimulate the nerves to regenerate slowly by stimulating the associated muscles. Usually electroacupuncture is used to stimulate contraction of the associated muscle and thus healing of the nerves. Both soft tissue structures and nerve damage respond better if treated soon after the injury, so acupuncture should be provided as soon as possible for the best results.

Examples of nerve damage that may respond to acupuncture are the following:

1) Sweeny — damage to a nerve that supplies the muscles of the shoulder

2) Radial nerve paralysis — inability to advance the limb without dragging the toe; the elbow appears dropped; usually caused by the horse "doing the splits" during a fall

3) Facial nerve paralysis — resulting in curvature of the lip to the side; usually secondary to an injury from the halter on the cheek

4) Traumatic wobblers — ataxia due to instability of the cervical vertebrae and impingement of the spinal cord; the

horse moves as if he/she has been sedated

5) Vestibular injuries — damage to the inner ear that usually results from the horse's rearing and flipping over.

Obviously a horse's response to acupuncture therapy depends on the severity of the trauma. All of the above conditions have responded positively to acupuncture treatments.

OLDER HORSES

Geriatric conditions such as Cushing's Disease and pituitary adenomas (tumors of the pituitary gland) can benefit from acupuncture. As discussed previously, needling can have dramatic effects on the hypothalamus-pituitary axis. Older horses also can have chronic arthritis. Acupuncture can make these animals significantly more comfortable and able to get around more easily. Acupuncture is useful for chronic pain because it can elicit memory loss in pain-receiving cells. When pain is long-standing, cells in the central nervous system store or memorize that pain signal. Once the memory is stored, it takes less noxious stimuli to elicit pain. Acupuncture reduces the pain signal by blocking the signal's transmission. In essence, it erases the memory in these pain-receiving cells. These cells are also activated by changes in barometric pressure. This helps explain why chronic pain, such as arthritis of the joints, is related to weather changes.

EYE PROBLEMS

Ophthalmic diseases also can be treated with acupuncture. These include corneal ulcers, conjunctivitis, and periodic ophthalmia (moon blindness). The Liver meridian opens to the eyes and is used for these conditions. Eye problems should always be treated with both conventional and alternative methods since the eye is such a delicate organ. Most horses are remarkably cooperative for needling sites around the eyes.

SHOCK

Acupuncture has a potent effect on arrhythmias and on

heart rate. In hemorrhagic shock, stimulation for 10 minutes of acupoint GV26 between the nostrils results in an increase in cardiac output, increased stroke volume, increased heart rate, increased mean arterial pressure, increased pulse pressure, and a decreased total peripheral resistance. These effects were observed for two hours after stimulation.

Dr. Jan Still, a research veterinarian, heavily anesthetized dogs and cats with phenobarbital, a commonly used anesthetic, to study the effects of acupuncture on cardiovascular shock. She observed how many animals treated with acupuncture survived compared to those treated with intravenous noradrenalin and those with no treatment. Seventy-five percent of those treated by needling GV26 alone survived compared to 80 percent that were treated traditionally with noradrenalin. Only 18 percent of the animals that were not treated at all survived. This illustrates that acupuncture can be just as effective as some Western methods of treatment. Other advantages of acupuncture for shock cases are its lack of expense, ease of administration, and extreme simplicity. It can be used immediately while emergency medications are being prepared and a catheter is being placed. This study suggests that acupuncture could help patients in shock or those that are heavily anesthetized and having difficulty recovering from anesthesia.

In a similar study, dogs

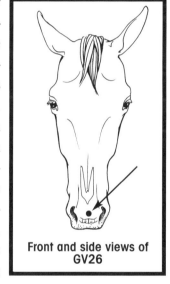

Front and side views of GV26

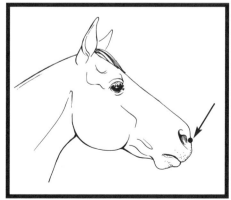

were given rabbit blood to induce anaphylactic shock. Any time an animal is treated with blood from another species, a severe reaction to the different blood types occurs. This is why human blood donors are tested for their blood type; humans are more sensitive than animals and react to human blood if it is a blood type different from their own. One group of dogs was treated with acupuncture only and 75 percent of those dogs lived. The other group was not treated at all and none of the dogs survived.

Acupoint GV26, located on the nose between the bottom of the nostrils, is also called the "anti-shock" point and the "life-saving" point. It is the best known and most used revival point in acupuncture and is an example of a point that has sympathomimetic effects, meaning it can stimulate the heart and lungs to increase their functions. Activation of this point affects the brain, heart, blood pressure, and respiration during resuscitation from shock. Stimulation of these organs enhances blood flow to the life support system and delivers oxygen to the brain and the heart. This is essential for resuscitation of an animal in shock. Endorphins and enkelphins are natural opiates that are released and help relieve pain.

Stimulation of GV26 has been used for several other purposes. The Finnish Lapps, who use reindeer as draught animals to pull sleighs, stimulate GV26 to revive reindeer that are exhausted by overexertion. This point has been used to treat shock in sows and rats. It has been used for hemorrhagic shock where the patient has lost large amounts of blood. It has been used to induce respiration and prevent brain damage from lack of oxygen in foals and calves that are not breathing when they are born. Strong needling of GV26 can resuscitate 90 to 100 percent of cases of simple apnea, or lack of breathing, in 10 to 30 seconds.

Acupoint ST36 also has sedative effects in cases of convulsion and mania. In humans only one side of the body is treated when needling ST36 because blood pressure drops following treatment.

ANALGESIA

Analgesia is the absence of pain or the sensibility to pain, such as the pain associated with surgery. Analgesia is most commonly achieved by inhalant or gas anesthesia in hospitals today. In the past acupuncture enabled surgeons in China to perform brain and heart surgery with analgesia at a time when general anesthesia had not been invented. Modern-day anesthetic agents are safe and have few side effects in the healthy patient. There may, however, be enormous advantages to combining acupuncture analgesia with modern day anesthetic agents. There is no loss of consciousness with acupuncture analgesia. Physiologic effects of acupuncture analgesia are rare as compared with injected or inhaled anesthetics. This may be important for patients that are geriatric or severely debilitated by disease. The most frequent observation in surgery performed with acupuncture analgesia is that less bleeding occurs, another factor that may be important in the compromised patient. Furthermore, acupuncture analgesia can reduce anesthetic doses, reduce post-operative pain, speed recovery, lessen swelling, and reduce the risk of aspiration. Aspiration is inhalation of fluids during the unconscious state that can lead to severe pneumonia.

Neurohumoral substances or neurotransmitters mediate acupuncture analgesia. The needles are placed and then either manually or electrically stimulated. Studies have shown that activation of acupoints for analgesia stimulate an area in the brain to send signals that inhibit the nerves carrying signals for painful stimuli down the spinal cord. In addition to specific neural pathways being activated, humoral substances play a role in acupuncture analgesia. This humoral response is evidenced by an experiment in which cerebral spinal fluid and blood samples were taken from donors undergoing acupuncture. The body fluids injected into the cerebral spinal space of recipient animals produced an analgesia in the recipients. The parasympathetic nervous system also has been implicated in acupuncture analgesia. Drugs that block the parasympathetic signal transmission will reduce the amount of acupuncture analgesia. Atropine, an anticholinergic drug, will reduce the amount of acupuncture analgesia.

CONTRAINDICATIONS

Acupuncture has numerous benefits and is a very safe therapy. There are, however, selected cases where acupuncture is contraindicated. As mentioned previously, acupuncture should not be performed on a horse that is being given or has recently received systemic corticosteroids. These medications may be appropriate for the disease, but they also will interfere with the positive effects of acupuncture.

Certain acupuncture points also can induce labor or cause abortions in pregnant subjects. Most human acupuncturists will not perform any type of acupuncture on pregnant women because of potential litigation. There are, to date, no reports of horses losing a pregnancy following acupuncture treatment. If careful point selection is used, it should be safe to use this therapy in pregnant mares. The author would discourage the use of electroacupuncture in pregnant mares unless it is used on the limbs. Positive results can be achieved by using a different modality, such as dry needling, without any possible risk to the pregnancy. The treatments may take longer to achieve the desired effect. There are even protocols to maintain pregnancy using dry needles. These protocols require monthly treatments of high-risk mares with dry needles left in place for 30 minutes. The therapy helps maintain good blood flow to the uterus and promote general health.

Acupuncture can sometimes fail to help an animal. A horse may not respond to acupuncture therapy for numerous reasons. If the treatment goal is not met, the practitioner should re-evaluate and try different treatments. The alternate treatments may simply be different acupoints or techniques or different medical or surgical interventions. If acupuncture is not helping the patient, the diagnosis should be reassessed. If the acupuncturist is treating a secondary problem, the problem is not likely to resolve without addressing the primary problem. For example, horses with lameness in the lower hind leg can experience secondary back pain. Acupuncture is a very good treatment for sore backs, but it is usually only a temporary resolution if the hocks or stifles have disease. The best therapy would be to treat the lower-leg problem appropriately and do the acupuncture to relieve the secondary back pain. Sore backs can also be caused by poor shoeing, faulty conformation, rider's position or ability, and poor saddle fit. Consider these factors when evaluating lameness.

There also may be pre-existing problems that prohibit the effects of acupuncture, such as neurogenic disease processes. Acupuncture is not able to work to its fullest because the nervous system is used to obtain a response. If the nervous system is damaged, some of the mechanisms of acupuncture may be blocked. Environmental factors and the horse's disposition also can affect the outcome of acupuncture therapy.

A horse that becomes agitated by the treatment sessions might hurt itself or the handler. This kind of stress cannot possibly be good for the animal. Therefore, the acupuncturist must use an alternative treatment.

The environment in which the horse is kept also can be relevant to the success of acupuncture. Practical management must not be forgotten. A horse with Chronic Obstructive Pulmonary Disease, commonly referred to as heaves, will not respond to acupuncture if he is kept in a poorly ventilated stall that is not mucked out regularly. Similarly, a horse with chronic navicular syndrome will not respond to acupuncture if his feet are not shod on a regular basis.

In summary, acupuncture is one of the most "field tested" techniques available in complementary medicine. Although there is no substitute for well-documented research using controlled clinical trials, thousands of years of clinical experience cannot be easily dismissed. Further research must be conducted to establish the maximum potential of acupuncture as a treatment modality.

CHAPTER 10

Cases Involving Acupuncture

The following are actual cases in which the author used acupuncture to treat an injury or condition. The patients ranged from foals and young horses to breeding animals and geriatrics.

RADIAL NERVE PARALYSIS

A four-year-old mare presented, dragging her left front leg and having difficulty advancing the limb. She had just been transported cross-country and it was suspected that she had received some type of shoulder joint injury on the trip. Radiographs of the shoulder and elbow were normal. She was diagnosed with radial nerve paralysis and given a very poor prognosis. She would not bear any weight on the affected limb, and there was great concern that the opposite leg would not be able to withstand all the weight. There was severe muscle atrophy surrounding the shoulder joint. She had been treated with steroids, anti-inflammatory agents, and antibiotics for one week with minimal response.

Acupuncture was started 12 days after the initial injury. She was treated for eight weeks with electroacupuncture applied across the shoulder joint, one to two times weekly. The meridians used were the Triple Heater, Small Intestine, Large Intestine, and Lung. She progressed rapidly and was eventually able to walk normally. She went on to become pregnant and deliver a normal, healthy foal the following year. I have treated numerous cases similar to this one with remarkable success. Most cases respond better if the therapy is started within a day or two of the injury.

CHRONIC LAMINITIS IN A PONY

A 28-year-old pony had had laminitis of varying degrees over the previous four years. She had deteriorated to the point that she was unable to get up on her own. She could stand for short periods of time only if she was assisted to her feet. She would get recurrent abscesses in her toe. She had been on anti-inflammatory agents, antibiotics, and isox-uprine. She also had had surgery to transect both of her front flexor tendons. This surgery reduces the tension or pull of the flexor tendon on the coffin bone to slow or stop the rotation of the coffin bone. The pony was treated with electroacupuncture along the Bladder meridian, vitamin B12 acupuncture at ST36 and the Spleen Association point, and dry needles in *Ting* points. She was able to get up on her own after four sessions in two weeks. Her attitude improved dramatically. She has been treated monthly for almost a year now. She has gained more than 100 pounds and does not get abscesses in her feet as often. She is growing healthy, normal hoof, and her coat has improved.

Laminitis is an extremely difficult condition to treat with Western medicine or Traditional Chinese Medicine. No two horses respond the same to any given treatment. Acupuncture can help to relieve the pain associated with the disease. It is not a "quick fix" and takes a great deal of patience. Some horses respond dramatically as this pony did; others do not respond well at all.

SEVERE STRINGHALT

An 18-year-old pregnant mare presented with acute, severe stringhalt of unknown origin. Stringhalt is a condition in which one or both hind legs move spastically as the horse walks. It may be so severe that a hind foot actually kicks the belly. Treatment usually involves surgery of the affected limb to transect and remove one of the tendons on the lateral aspect of the hock. The owners did not want to risk an older mare or the pregnancy by using general anesthesia to perform surgery. The mare was treated for Excess Wind with electroacupuncture applied to the gluteal area. All signs of stringhalt disappeared after four treatments in two weeks. She was not treated with any other medications. I have treated six cases similar to this, and each has responded well. Most cases take four to six treatments.

CHRONIC NAVICULAR DISEASE

A 10-year-old show horse was diagnosed with navicular disease, based on nerve blocks and radiographic abnormalities in the navicular bone. The horse was chronically lame in alternating front feet. The horse was initially treated with corrective shoeing, occasional anti-inflammatory agents, and oral isoxuprine. He was sound and able to perform well for more than a year. He then started to have intermittent bouts of lameness that progressively worsened despite therapy. The owner decided to try acupuncture for the lameness. Three electroacupuncture sessions were done on the heel region of both front feet. The horse was sound without medication for just over one year. At this time the lameness returned, and the horse was treated again with three acupuncture sessions. He again was sound for approximately eight months. He was then retired and remained sound for pasture turnout.

CHRONIC DIARRHEA IN FOALS

A three-month-old foal had diarrhea for four weeks. The foal was not clinically ill from the diarrhea, but it was not thriving. The foal had been treated with antibiotics, anti-ulcer medication, fluids, probiotics, and oral electrolytes. The diarrhea persisted. The foal was treated once with two to three cc of vitamin B12 injected into an acupoint on the Large Intestine meridian. Vitamin B12 was used to allow longer stimulation of the acupoint than with dry needling. The diarrhea resolved within 24 hours and did not return. I just started using acupuncture to treat foals with chronic diarrhea this year (2001). I have treated eight foals, and all have responded impressively.

INAPPETENCE/GASTROINTESTINAL ULCERS

A two-year-old racehorse presented with inappetence and mild recurring colic, especially after eating. An endoscopic examination of the horse's stomach showed severe ulcers in the lining. The horse was treated with anti-ulcer medication, and the ulcers improved. However, if the medication was stopped even for one day, the signs returned and the horse would colic. The horse was treated with acupuncture using dry needles and vitamin B12 aquapuncture in acupoints associated with the Stomach meridian. Several studies have shown that acupuncture can significantly reduce stomach acidity, thus reducing the formation of ulcers. After four treatments the horse started to perform better. The client was able to discontinue the medications and maintain the ulcers with acupuncture treatment every two weeks. The anti-ulcer medication is given only on race days. An endoscopic examination one month after the medications were stopped showed a normal, healthy lining of the stomach. The horse's appetite returned to normal.

BROODMARES WITH URINE POOLING OR UTERINE FLUID

I have treated hundreds of mares that retain fluid in the uterus during estrus and/or after breeding. Older mares in particular seem to have trouble clearing normal fluid produced during estrus and in response to breeding. The fluid is noticeable on rectal ultrasound examinations. The treatment involves electroacupuncture with three coated wires, or leads, from the sacrum to the top of the tail. Occasionally, moxibustion is used on an acupoint on the Bladder meridian that is associated with reproduction. Vitamin B12 acupuncture is also sometimes indicated to treat points associated with infertility and well-being such as Spleen 9 and Stomach 36. Referring veterinarians comment that they are able to palpate a "tighter" or "firmer" uterus on rectal palpation within 24 hours of the treatment. Most of the horses I treat have already been treated with oxytocin, prostaglandins, antibiotics, and uterine infusions without clinical improvement.

POST-FOALING BLADDER PARALYSIS

An eight-year-old mare presented with bladder paralysis after delivering her first foal. She was completely raw from urine scald all down the inside of her hind legs. She had been treated with anti-inflammatory agents and antibiotics, but had not improved after three weeks of treatment. The medications were stopped, and she was treated with electroacupuncture along the Bladder meridian. Chinese herbs were administered orally. She improved dramatically and got in foal that season. These cases respond best if the acupuncture is started soon after the insult.

FAILURE TO CYCLE NORMALLY

A Thoroughbred mare had not shown signs of estrus for more than three years although she had produced foals previously. She was treated with aquapuncture and dry needles. Certain hormones were injected directly into acupoints associated with fertility on the Bladder meridian. The mare was treated every other day for three treatments. She showed a normal estrus in 10 days. She went through a normal estrous cycle and showed normal estrus in the following cycle. She went on to get in foal on the second cycle.

DECREASED LIBIDO IN STALLIONS

A stallion presented one month into the breeding season for decreased libido. He was reluctant to mount mares and would take a long time to breed, if he would breed at all. He was treated with hormone therapy for one month, and the problem worsened. He then was treated with electroacupuncture three times a week for two weeks. He responded well and is still treated monthly. Some stallions show reduced libido because their backs or hocks are sore. These cases also respond to acupuncture treatment.

CHAPTER 11

Herbal Treatments

Approximately 85 percent of the world's population use herbs. Many people try herbal medicine before prescription medicine or use the two concurrently. In fact, many modern drugs were originally derived from compounds isolated in plants.

The Egyptians first cultivated medicinal plants. The Greek physician Hippocrates in the fifth century B.C. used powder extracted from the bark of willow trees to treat pain and reduce fever. More recent research revealed willow bark contained salicin. Today, a refinement of this substance is known as aspirin and is synthesized into tablets. Aspirin is related to the herb white willow, and anti-ulcer medications are very similar to the herb licorice. Steroids have properties very similar to wild yam.

Herbal therapy is termed phytotherapy and is based on a plant's natural ability to heal. In China acupuncture and herbs are almost always used together (see chapter 6). Veterinary herbal remedies were used more commonly when fewer treatment options were available. Hundreds of herbal remedies are still on the market today and are usually very affordable and very safe.

Herbs usually work in one of three ways. Several act by provoking a response. These include expectorants (agents that help the body clear mucus from the lungs), diuretics (agents that work on the kidneys to increase water excretion), astringents (agents that cause contraction after topical application), and demulcents (topical agents that soothe irritated surfaces such as the skin). Other herbs act as normalizers to increase or decrease a particular function such as circulation. The third group of herbs acts as eliminators or cleansers to rid the body of toxins. Herbs have trace minerals and enzymes that act as catalysts to stimulate cell regeneration. Herbs can come in different forms: fresh herbs, powders, and brewed teas. The dose depends on the size of the animal and the duration of the condition. Acute conditions usually require a higher dose at frequent intervals. Chronic conditions require more long-term treatment at a lower dose.

Herbal therapies are prescribed for many ailments or problems. Topically, they can be particularly helpful on wounds, reducing the inflammation and increasing local circulation. Herbal treatments are used for geriatric horses as well as for horses with exercise-induced pulmonary hemorrhage, fertility problems and systemic diseases and topically on bowed tendons. An excellent report in the *Journal of Equine Veterinary Science* (Xie, H et al. "Chinese Herbal Medicine for Equine Acute Diarrhea," Vol. 19, No. 4, 1999) discusses the efficacy of herbal medicine for equine acute diarrhea.

Owners interested in using herbal products on their horses should consult with a specialist and their veterinarian because of the myriad of natural supplements on the market. Professionals are rapidly researching several of these therapies. There is now a *Physicians Desk Reference For Herbal Medicine*. The best results are obtained when a trained practitioner conducts a TCM examination to make a proper diagnosis. Remember that even though herbal remedies are "natural," they are not always indicated in certain conditions. It can be dangerous to mix herbs inappropriately or use an herb with prescription medications.

GLOSSARY

Acupuncture — The Chinese practice of insertion of needles into specific exterior body locations to relieve pain and to induce surgical anesthesia, and for therapeutic purposes.

ACTH — Adrenocorticotropic hormone. A peptide hormone secreted by the anterior pituitary gland that acts primarily on the adrenal cortex, stimulating its growth and secretion of corticosteroids. The production of corticotropin is increased by stress.

Adenoma — A benign epithelial tumor in which the cells form recognizable glandular structures or in which the cells are clearly derived from glandular epithelium or lining.

Adrenal gland — A flattened body situated at the cranial pole of the kidney. The adrenal cortex, under control of the pituitary hormone corticotropin, produces steroid hormones — glucocorticoids, mineralocorticoids, androgens, and progestins. The adrenal medulla produces the catecholamines, epinephrine, and norepinephrine.

Afferent nerve — A nerve conveying sensations such as heat, cold, pain, rough, soft, etc.to the brain.

Anaphylaxis — A manifestation of immediate hypersensitivity in which exposure to a specific antigen or hapten results in life-threatening respiratory distress usually followed by vascular collapse and shock.

Arrhythmia — Any variation from the normal rhythm of the heart beat.

Atony — Lack of normal tone or strength.

Autonomic nervous system — The portion of the nervous system that regulates activity of heart muscle, smooth muscle (uterus and gastrointestinal tract), and glands.

Bone spavin — Osteoperiostitis or arthritis of the intertarsal or tarsometatarsal articulation (hock joint).

Bradycardia — Slowness of the heart beat.

Central nervous system — The portion of the nervous system consisting of the brain and spinal cord.

Chiropractic — A science of applied neurophysiologic diagnosis based on the theory that health and disease are life processes related to the function of the nervous system. Irritation of the nervous system by mechanical, chemical, or psychic factors is the cause of disease; restoration and maintenance of health depend on normal function of the nervous system. Diagnosis is the identification of these noxious irritants, and treatment is their removal by the most conservative method.

Colic — Acute abdominal pain.

Corticosteroids — Any of the body's natural steroids produced by the adrenal gland (a small gland that is next to the kidney) in response to the release of corticotrophin (ACTH hormone) by the pituitary gland.

Cortisol — The body's major natural steroid produced by the adrenal cortex.

Cryptorchid — A developmental defect characterized by failure of the testes to descend into the scrotum.

Cushing's Disease — Chronic elevation of the hormone cortisol. In the horse it presents as a horse that does not shed its coat properly, drinks a lot, has chronic feet abscesses and an enlarged crest of the neck.

Cystitis — Inflammation of the urinary bladder.

Degenerative joint disease — Osteoarthritis, which is a non-inflammatory degenerative joint disease occurring chiefly in older individuals, characterized by degeneration of the articular cartilage, hypertrophy of the bone at margins, and changes in the synovial membranes. Pain and stiffness accompany it, particularly after prolonged activity.

Dermatosis — Inflammation of the skin.

DMSO — Dimethyl sulfoxide is an alkyl sulfoxide. Its biologic activities include the ability to penetrate plant and animal tissues and to preserve living cells during freezing. It has been used as a topical anti-inflammatory agent and as an agent to increase the penetrability of other substances

Efferent nerve — Any nerve that carries impulses from the central nervous system toward the periphery or to muscles, as a motor nerve.

Endogenous — Developing or originating within the organism, or arising from the causes within the organism.

Erythema — A name applied to redness of the skin produced by congestion of the capillaries, which may result from a variety of causes.

Estrus — The recurrent, restricted period of sexual receptivity in female mammals other than human females, marked by intense sexual urge.

Histamine — A product found in all body tissues, particularly in mast cells and their related blood basophils, the highest concentration being in the lungs. It is also present in ergot and other plants and may be synthesized outside the body from histidine or citric acid. It has several functions, including (1) dilation of capillaries, which increases capillary permeability and results in a drop of blood pressure; (2) contraction of most smooth muscle tissue, including bronchial smooth muscle of the lung; (3) induction of increased gastric secretion; and (4) acceleration of the heart rate.

Homeostasis — A tendency toward stability in the normal body states (internal environment) of any living being. It is achieved by a system of control mechanisms activated by negative feedback.

Humoral — Pertaining to elements dissolved in the blood or body fluids.

Hypothalamus — Anatomically, it includes the preoptic area, optic tract, optic chiasm, mamillary bodies, tuber cinereum, infundibulum, and neurohypophysis. The hypothalamic nuclei regulate body processes through the production of hormones or control of nerve cells.

Ileus — Obstruction or lack of movement of the intestines.

Inappetence — Lack of desire or appetite.

Laminitis — Inflammation of the laminae of the hoof wall.

Laser — A device that transforms light of various frequencies into an extremely intense, small, and nearly non-divergent beam of radiation. Capable of mobilizing heat and power when focused at close range.

Libido — Sexual desire.

Luteolysis — Degeneration of corpus luteum.

Mast cells — A connective tissue cell whose specific physiologic function is to release histamine and initiate vasodilatation.

Meridian — An imaginary line on the surface of a spherical body. In Traditional Chinese Medicine it is also referred to as a channel.

Metritis — Inflammation of the uterus.

Moxa — A Chinese herb, *Artemisia vulgaris*, commonly called mugwort, that is processed into a cylindrical shape and used in moxibustion.

Moxibustion — Counterirritation produced by igniting a cone or cylinder of moxa placed on the skin.

Navicular syndrome — Chronic pain in the heel region of the hoof.

Neoplasia — The formation of a cancer; the progressive multiplication of cells under conditions that would not elicit, or would cause cessation of, multiplication of normal cells.

Nephritis — Inflammation of the kidney, a focal or diffuse proliferative or destructive process that may involve the glomerulus, tubule, or interstitial renal tissue.

Nerve — A cord-like structure, visible to the naked eye, comprising a collection of nerve fibers that conveys impulses between a part of the central nervous system and some other region of the body.

Neurohormones — A hormone stimulating the neural mechanism.

Neuropathy — A general term denoting functional disturbances and/or pathological changes in the peripheral nervous system.

Nuclear scintigraphy — The production of two-dimensional images of the distribution of radioactivity in tissues after the internal administration of radionucleotide, the images being obtained by a scintillation camera.

Opioids — Any synthetic narcotic that has opiate-like activities but is not derived from opium. Denoting naturally occurring peptides, e.g., enkephalins, that exert opiate-like effects by interacting with opiate receptors of cell membranes.

Orchitis — Inflammation of the testis.

Paraphimosis — Retraction of phimotic foreskin, causing a painful swelling of the glans and the inability to retract the penis.

Parasympathetic nervous system — The part of the autonomic nervous system that controls unconscious bodily functions such as digestion, urination, and defecation.

Pituitary gland — A gland at the base of the brain that regulates the secretion of hormones.

Prostaglandin — Any of a group of components derived from arachidonic acid, via the cyclooxygenase pathway, that are extremely potent mediators of a diverse group of physiologic process, especially inflammation.

Pylorus — The last portion of the stomach, surrounded by a strong band of circular muscle and through which the stomach contents are emptied into the duodenum.

Pyometra — An accumulation of pus in the uterus.

Qi — The force or energy that controls harmony in the body.

Ringbone — A bony growth involving the first or second phalanx of the foot, resulting in lameness if the articular surfaces are affected.

Serapin — An aqueous solution from the pitcher plant (*Sarraceniaceae*) that selectively blocks the C fibers that carry pain sensation in peripheral nerves.

Sidebone — A condition of horses marked by ossification of the lateral cartilages of the third phalanx of the foot.

Somatic — Pertaining to the characteristic of the soma or body;

pertaining to the body wall in contrast to the viscera.

Somatotropin — Growth hormone.

Sweeny — Shoulder slip. Shoulder damage historically caused by the neck collar used in plow horses.

Sympathetic nervous system — The portion of the autonomic nervous system responsible for the "fight or flight" mechanism. This nervous system allows an animal to run when scared.

Synapse — The site of functional apposition between neurons at which an impulse is transmitted from one neuron to another by electrical or chemical means.

Tachycardia — Excessive rapidity in the action of the heart.

Thermography — A technique in which an infrared camera is used to show the surface temperatures of the body, based on the self-emanating infrared radiation; sometimes employed as a means of diagnosing underlying pathologic processes, such as breast tumors.

Trigger points — A particular spot on the body on which pressure or other stimuli will give rise to specific sensations or symptoms.

Vestibular — Pertaining to or toward the vestibule, which is a space or cavity at the entrance to a canal, usually the ear canal.

INDEX

RECOMMENDED READINGS

Cain, M. (Donahue, N. ed.) *Acupuncture Diagnosis and Treatment of the Equine.* 3rd edition. Corrales, NM: BioScan Inc. 1996.

Kaptchuk, TJ. *The Web That Has No Weaver.* New York: Congdon & Weed. 1983.

Pinsi, A. *Acupuncture for Horses.* 8th edition. Bronxville, NY: The Able Body. 1998.

Sellnow, L. "Use and Abuse of Natural Products," *The Horse*, Vol. 17, No. 6, p. 29-30, 32-34, 36, 40-42, June 2000.

Sellnow, L. "Acupuncture Part I; Ancient Art, Modern Healing," *The Horse*, p. 14-20, January 1997.

Sellnow, L. "Acupuncture Part II; Acupuncture as a Diagnostic," *The Horse*, p. 55-60, February 1997.

Sellnow, L. "Acupuncture Part III; Acupuncture as a Therapy," *The Horse*, p. 63-70, March 1997.

Schoen, AM. "Ancient Art to Modern Medicine," *Veterinary Acupuncture*, p. 543-549, 1994.

Schoen, AM. "Equine Acupuncture: Incorporation into Lameness Diagnosis and Treatment," Proceedings of the American Association of Equine Practitioners, Vol. 41, p. 135-137, 1995.

Snader, ML., et al. *Healing Your Horse*, p. 3-208. New York: Macmillan General Reference. 1993.

In 1988 the American Veterinary Medicine Association declared that "veterinary acupuncture and acutherapy are considered valid modalities, but the potential for abuse exists. These techniques should be regarded as surgical and/or medical procedures under state practice acts. It is recommended that extensive continuing educational programs be undertaken before a veterinarian is considered competent to practice acupuncture."

If you want to consult with an acupuncturist for your horse, you should use a licensed veterinarian that is certified in acupuncture by the International Veterinary Acupuncture Society (IVAS). A licensed veterinarian is in the best position to diagnose the animal's health problem and determine if the horse will benefit from acupuncture or whether it needs other treatment modalities. You should talk to your regular veterinarian and discuss all treatment options.

Only veterinarians are admitted into the certification program offered by IVAS. The certification program requires veterinarians to complete a five-day, four-session intensive study of veterinary acupuncture. It also requires that the veterinarian pass a written and practical examination, write a clinical case report, and study under a certified acupuncturist for a set number of hours. IVAS is a non-profit organization that is dedicated to promoting excellence in the practice of veterinary acupuncture as an integral part of the total veterinary health care delivery system. The organization has annual educational programs and requires continuing education for its members. IVAS is the primary source of educational programs outside of China. It also promotes and supports further investigation and research in veterinary acupuncture.

For more information on an acupuncturist in your area, contact IVAS:

International Veterinary Acupuncture Society
P.O. Box 271395
Fort Collins, CO 80527
Phone: 970-266-0666; Fax: 970-266-0777

The Association of British Veterinary Acupuncturists (ABVA)
East Park Cottage, Handcross
Haywards Heath, West Sussex RH17 6BD
United Kingdom

Acupuncture on the Internet

The American Academy of Veterinary Acupuncture:
www.aava.org

Equine Studies Institute: www.equinestudies.org

Equine Veterinary Network: www.equinevetnet.com

The Holistic Horse: www.holistichorse.com

The Horse: Your Guide to Equine Health Care magazine:
www.thehorse.com

The International Veterinary Acupuncture Society:
www.ivas.org

International Veterinary Acupuncture Directory:
www.komvet.at/ivadkom/vapsocs.htm

Pacific Coast Equine Acupuncture and Alternative Medicine:
www.equineacupuncture.com

REFERENCES

"The I.V.A.S. Veterinary Acupuncture Course Notes," The International Veterinary Acupuncture Society, Longmont, CO, Vol. 7, 1998.

Bryant, JO. "Alternative Therapies: Quality or Quackery?" *The Horse*, Vol. 17, No. 6, p. 45-46, 48, 50-54, June 2000.

Bryant, JO. "Selecting an Alternative Practitioner," *The Horse*, Vol. 17, No. 6, p. 43-44, June 2000.

Cain, M. (Donahue, N. ed.) *Acupuncture Diagnosis and Treatment of the Equine*. 3rd Edition. Corrales, NM: BioScan Inc. 1996.

Cerovsky, J et al. "Acupuncture to Induce Oestrus in Gilts," *Research Institute of Animal Production*, p. 1-4, July 2, 2000.

Cho, ZH. "New findings of the correlation between acupoints and corresponding brain cortices using functional MRI," Proceedings of the National Academy of Sciences, Vol. 95, p. 2670-2673, March 1998.

DeRock, JL. "Crookedness In The Horse." www.equineacupuncture.com/learning.html. p. 1-5, October 27, 2000.

Dill, SG et al. "Cardiovascular Effects of Acupuncture Stimulation at Point Governing Vessel 26 in Halothane-anesthetized Ponies," *American Journal of Veterinary Research*, Vol. 49, No. 10, p. 1708-1712, October 1988.

Ernst, E. (Ed.) "Acupuncture, Fools, and Horses," *Journal of Pain and Symptom Management*, Vol. 14, No. 6, p. 325-326, December 1997.

Gideon, L. "Acupuncture: Clinical Trials in the Horse," *JAVMA*, Vol. 170, No. 2, January 15, 1977.

Gunn, C. *Treating Myofascial Pain*. Seattle, WA: University of Washington Press, p. 7-14, 1989.

Hao, LC. "Electroacupuncture Therapy Trial for Treating Infertility In Mares," *Theriogenology*, Vol. 28, No. 3, p. 301-305, September 1987.

Harman, JC. "Backs, Performance, and Acupuncture," Proceedings of the American Association of Equine Practitioners, p. 337-347, 1992.

Harman, JC. "Quick Introduction to Acupuncture," *Equine Practice*, Vol. 18, No. 5, p. 33-34, May 1996.

Hilsenroth, R. "Acupuncture and Treatment of Back Pain in Horses," *Equine Practice*, Vol. 20, No. 8, p. 24, September 1998.

Hoogenraad, RG. "Equine Ataxia," *International Journal of Veterinary Acupuncture*, Vol. 8, No. 2, p. 11-13, July-December 1997.

Jagger, DH. "History and Concepts of Veterinary Acupuncture." In Schoen, A. *Veterinary Acupuncture: Ancient Art to Modern Medicine.* St. Louis: Mosby-Yearbook, p. 5-18, 1994.

Jenerick, HP. "Effect of Acupuncture," Proceedings of the NIH Acupuncture Research Conference, p. 106-107, February 28-March 1, 1973.

Jin, Y. *Handbook of Obstetrics and Gynecology in Chinese Medicine.* Seattle, WA: Eastland Press. 1998.

Jones, AH. "Energy Crisis: Eastern methods winning Western converts," *The Mane Points*, p. 3-5, Winter 2001.

Kendall, DE. "Part I: A Scientific Model for Acupuncture," *American Journal of Acupuncture*, Vol. 17, No. 3, p. 251-268, July-September 1989.

Kendall, DE. "Part II: A Scientific Model for Acupuncture," *American Journal of Acupuncture*, Vol. 17, No. 4, p. 343-360, 1989.

Klide, AM. "Use of Acupuncture for the Control of Chronic Pain and for Surgical Analgesia," *Animal Pain*, p. 249-257, 1992.

Klide, AM and Benson, BM. "Methods of stimulating acupuncture points for treatment of chronic back pain in horses," *JAVMA*, Vol. 195, No. 10, p. 1375-1379, November 15, 1989.

Landholm, JE. "Use of Acupuncture in Treatment of Laminitis in a Horse," *Veterinary Medicine/Small Animal Clinician*, p. 405-407, March 1981.

Leimbach, J. "Healing Horses: Equine Sports Therapy," *The Horsemen's Journal*, p. 28-30, May 1999.

Lin, JH et al. "Acupuncture Treatments for Animal Reproductive Disorders." Department of Animal Science, National Taiwan University, Republic of China. http://users.med.auth.gr.

Lischer, CJ. "Acupuncture Treatment of Radial Nerve Paralysis In A Cow," *International Journal of Veterinary Acupuncture*, Vol. 8, No. 2, p. 5-7, July-December 1997.

Lopez, HS et al. "Pharmacologic and Alternative Therapies For The Horse With Chronic Laminitis," *Veterinary Clinics of North America: Equine Practice*, Vol. 15, No. 2, p. 495-517, August 1999.

Martin Jr., BB and Klide, AM. "Acupuncture for the Treatment of Chronic Back Pain in 200 Horses," Proceedings of the American Association of Equine Practitioners, Vol. 37, p. 593-601, 1991.

Martin Jr., BB and Klide, AM. "Use of acupuncture for the treatment of chronic back pain in horses: Stimulation of acupuncture points with saline solution injections," *JAVMA*, Vol. 190, No. 9, p. 1177-1180, May 1, 1987.

Matsumoto, T et al., Hayes Jr., MF. "Acupuncture, Electric Phenomenon of the Skin, and Postvagotomy Gastrointestinal Atony," *The American Journal of Surgery*, p. 176-180, 125 (2), 1972.

McCormick, WH. "Oriental Channel Diagnosis In Foot Lameness of the Equine Forelimb," *Journal of Equine Veterinary Science*, Vol. 17, No. 6, 1997.

McCormick, WH. "The Distribution of Meridian Imbalance in Metacarpo-Phalangeal Joint Dysfunction in the Horse," personal correspondence.

McCormick, WH. "The Origins of Acupuncture Channel Imbalance In Pain of the Equine Hindlimb," *Journal of Equine Veterinary Science*, Vol. 18, No. 8, 1998.

McCormick, WH. "The Use of Implants in the Treatment of Gall Bladder Channel Imbalance in the Horse, a Review of 114 Cases." Proceedings of the 20th Annual International Congress on Veterinary Acupuncture, 1994.

McIntyre, MB. "Ting Point Therapy in Exertional Rhabdomyolysis in a Dressage Horse," *International Journal of Veterinary Acupuncture*, Vol. 8, No. 2, p. 14-16, July-December, 1997.

Meehan, SK. "AAEP acupuncture lecture gets point across," *JAVMA*, Vol. 208, No. 3, p. 325-326, February 1, 1996.

Messonnier, S. "Current Theories of Acupuncture," *Veterinary*

Practice News, Vol. 13, No. 4, p. 32, April 2001.

Mittleman, E. and Gaynor, JS. "A brief overview of the analgesic and immunologic effects of acupuncture in domestic animals," *JAVMA,* Vol. 217, No. 8, p. 1201-1205, October 15, 2000.

O'Connor, J and Bensky, D. "A Summary of Research Concerning the Effects of Acupuncture," *American Journal of Chinese Medicine,* Vol. 3, No. 4, p. 377-394, 1975.

Patton, M. "Therapeutic Options Task Force Report," AAEP REPORT, p. 3-4, November 2000.

Pinsi, A. *Acupuncture for Horses.* 8th ed. Bronxville, NY: The Able Body, 1998.

Ramey, DW and Raso, J. "Horsefeathers: Acupuncture from a Veterinary Perspective," *Acupuncture and Alternative Therapies in the Horse,* Fall 1999.

Reynes, A. "Another Tool," *The Horse,* p. 55, January 2001.

Ridgway, K. "Acupuncture As A Treatment Modality For Back Problems," *Veterinary Clinics of North American: Equine Practice,* Vol. 15, No. 1, p. 211-221, April 1999.

Schoen, AM. "Ancient Art to Modern Medicine," *Veterinary Acupuncture,* p. 543-549, 1994.

Schoen, AM. "Equine Acupuncture: Incorporation into Lameness Diagnosis and Treatment," Proceedings of the American Association of Equine Practitioners, Vol. 41, p. 135-137, 1995.

Schoen, AM. "A Scientific Approach to Equine Acupuncture," *Let's Get To The Point,* p. 1-5, October 27, 2000.

Sellnow, L. "Use and Abuse of Natural Products," *The Horse,* Vol. 17, No. 6, p. 29-30, 32-34, 36, 40-42, June 2000.

Sellnow, L. "Acupuncture Part I: Ancient Art, Modern Healing," *The Horse,* p. 14-20, January 1997.

Sellnow, L. "Acupuncture Part II: Acupuncture as a Diagnostic," *The Horse,* p. 55-60, February 1997.

Sellnow, L. "Acupuncture Part III: Acupuncture as a Therapy," *The Horse,* p. 63-70, March 1997.

Snader, ML et al. *Healing Your Horse.* New York: Macmillan General Reference, p. 3-208, 1993.

Tickert, CG. "A Natural Approach to IBD," *Veterinary Practice News*, Vol. 13, No. 6, p. 27, June 2001.

Walsh, J. "Reversal of Post Colic Operational Side Effects Using Acupuncture," *International Journal of Veterinary Acupuncture*, Vol. 8, No. 1, p. 10-11, January-June 1997.

Westman, C. "Gold Bead Implants in Horses; Sixteen Cases," *International Journal of Veterinary Acupuncture*, Vol. 8, No. 1, p. 7, January-June 1997.

Wu, MT And Hsieh, JC. "Central Nervous Pathway for Acupuncture Stimulation: Localization of Processing with Functional MR Imaging of the Brain—Preliminary Experience," *Radiology*, p. 133-141, July 1999.

Xie, H et al., "Equine Chronic Diarrhea: Traditional Chinese Veterinary Medicine Review," *Journal of Equine Veterinary Science*, Vol. 17, No. 12, p. 667-674, 1997.

Xie, H et al., "A Review of the Use of Acupuncture for Treatment of Equine Back Pain," *Journal of Equine Veterinary Science*, Vol. 16, No. 7, p. 258-290, 1996.

Xie, H et al., "Chinese Herbal Medicine For Equine Acute Diarrhea," *Journal of Equine Veterinary Science*, Vol. 19, November 4, 1999.

Picture Credits

Anne M. Eberhardt, 62, 65, 70-72; Tom Hall, 18, 66-71
Illustrations: Robin Peterson

About the Author

 Rhonda Rathgeber, PhD, DVM, has been around horses most of her life. Growing up, she was active in the United States Pony Club and the 4-H Horse Program. She continued her involvement with horses through the pursuit of a veterinary medicine degree. She received a bachelor of science degree in microbiology in 1988 from the University of Florida, Gainesville. In 1992, she earned her Ph.D. in veterinary science and anatomy at Washington State University, and three years later, received her Doctor of Veterinary Medicine from the Virginia-Maryland Regional College of Veterinary Medicine. From there, she went to well-known equine hospital Hagyard-Davidson-McGee in Lexington, Kentucky, where she works as an equine associate veterinarian with special interest in lameness, ultrasound, and radiology.

Acupuncture is a large part of her practice, and Rathgeber is IVAS Certified in veterinary acupuncture. She also is a board member of the Thoroughbred Retirement Foundation and Central Kentucky Riding for the Handicapped; participates in the American Association of Equine Practitioners "On Call" Media Coverage program; and lectures for the University of Kentucky Animal Science Equine Management course.

Rathgeber has written or co-written 10 publications, and contributed to the video *First Aid for Horses*, produced by The Blood-Horse, Inc. She lives in Lexington.

The Horse Health Care Library